Tai Chi

It's Tai Chi Jim But Not As We Know It!

Howard Gibbon

ACKNOWLEDGMENTS

To my wonderful wife, who has been so patient with my often pushy demands. Her editing help, along with her insight and wisdom, are an invaluable aid to my writing aspirations. Thank you for being who you are, my life is enriched because of your presence on my journey.

Thanks must also go to Nic Bravin, who helped with the editing too. Nick has given me much support and encouragement over the years, for the work I do, to pass on our invaluable Arts we are custodians of.

Howard F Gibbon

CONTENTS

Introduction

If you are on a mission to discover the true depth of Tai Chi, then you will find much to interest you within these pages.

There are no techniques, no strange sounding names, no chest pounding. Instead, you are invited to seek the wisdom within. Presented as a collection of articles, in which Howard shares his understanding gleaned from his own experience of practising Tai Chi and related arts since 1973.

A collection of thoughts, arising from everyday occurrences that bubbled up from deep within. As he saw, with eyes imbued with knowledge, gained from countless hours of Tai Chi practice.

Like mankind can use chaos theory to explore outward, deep into space, and quantum physics to explore deep within the atom. So too does Tai Chi have an outer area of learning, but also contains an inner understanding that is only gained by those prepared to dig deep and venture far.

This wisdom changes the practitioner. Giving palpable physical skills, as well as mental attributes that assembles the world into a more enjoyable and beautiful place to be. The most benefit will be derived from reading each chapter more than once, and then allowing your own thought processes, to go to work on the information given.

The practise of Tai Chi has given me so much that I feel duty bound to offer what I can to others, who are seekers of truth.

For me, learning these arts has been like peeling an onion. Each time I stripped back a layer, there had been another underneath, and oftentimes as I peeled it away, it brought tears to my eyes.

To all of you, who have the courage and self discipline to reach for the stars and explore the depth of space, to go where others fear to tread. I salute you, in anticipation of your journey.

Through the struggles you will undoubtedly encounter, you will gain a wisdom that enhances your life. This process draws a beauty to your existence, that allows you to add your special talent to the pot of human kind.

For you are unique. There is no other like you, and there never will be another like you in the future. Allow yourself to create an exquisite life, so you, will be an example to others.

And remember that the journey never stops. A river is no longer a river, if it stops flowing. The wind, so necessary to the health of our eco system, is no longer the wind if it ceases to move.

Be not afraid of change; for there is no life without it.

I wish you all I wish for myself.

Howard

~~~

Tai Chi, Saviour of My Sanity

It is not often I experience a feeling of being totally overwhelmed, but a few days ago I woke feeling this way. Probably you have had the same feeling yourself sometime. There were family health issues, disputes and unhappiness in abundance. I had a DVD to finish, that had had its share of technical problems. I had a newsletter to get out in a few days. Admin work was piling up on my desk. Decisions to be make over course dates. The list went on and on...

It was 10.30am. I had answered phone calls and dealt with urgent emails already. But 1 had not done my regular Tai Chi practise yet.

My wife called out as I passed her office, and asked me to help her with a small task. I had to stop myself barking a reply. Something on the lines of I am too busy.

I was stressed, What? No, not me, surely? An experienced Tai Chi teacher, with many years under my belt, teaching other people how to bring peace and harmony into their lives.

Am I a hypocrite?

Should I not, be above all that sort of thing? Well Tai Chi is a tool, not a panacea for all ills of the body and mind. Tai Chi is no quick fix and like all tools, it is only useful when it is put to use.

Time for my Tai Chi practice.

I stepped out into our back garden onto the patio, my usual exercise place. As I looked down, to check I was standing on the correct spot, I noticed a ladybird to my front. It looked quite dead; I considered that I had probably, in my poor mental state, plagued with so many problems, stood on it, as I walked onto the patio. Out of dejection and irritation I, gently mind you, flicked it toward the grass with the edge of my shoe. It slid towards the grass, rolling over twice in the process, and then to my surprise, came alive and started walking back towards the spot I had just expelled it from.

Now my focus turned, to the safety of this ladybird. It was still full of life, heading back to its original spot, at a fair number of knots. Filled with remorse for the treatment I had given it, I looked around and noticed a dead leaf, which had fallen off the ivy climbing our garden fence. I picked it up and tenderly placed it, in the path of the ladybird and when it crawled onto the leaf, lifted it and placed it amongst the ivy.

Now feeling a little better about myself, I set to work on my Tai Chi practise. And work it turned out to be, because my mind was still consumed with my worries and waiting tasks. I persevered, completing the Tai Chi long form. This was not the real Tai Chi I had come to know, after many years of dedicated practise. This was mere, mechanical movement. My mind slipped in and out of attentiveness, drifting back and forth, from my movements to my problems and concerns and back again, to my practice. This was the way I used to perform my Tai Chi, in my early years. It had its value in the physical exercise and the brief moments of clarity, when I was focused on my Tai Chi. In touch with my physical reality, at the very moment of its conception. Then I quickly lost that connectedness again, as my mind moved too far in front, to think of a forthcoming movement or returned to one gone and analysed it. Both pastimes fruitless, for the future having not yet arrived and the past having gone, forever, never to return.

I performed the Tai Chi long form a second and third time, in this very state. Exercising my body, no doubt moving my energy, in a sluggish kind of way, and struggling to control my thought processes.

Then suddenly, remarkable quickly, everything fell into place. The physical flow, that place I have come to know where, I become the watcher and the watched, my being in harmony, body, mind and spirit working together as one, no separation only the essence of being. No more distractions, no more disturbances. The muddy waters now clear and calm. I continued my Tai Chi practise clocking up 1 hour and 10 minutes, more than twice my usual training time for the Tai Chi form and I wanted to go on. It felt so good, I did not want it to end. But I knew that balance, must be the overruling principle. So I stopped my practise, now calm in spirit and smiling at the ladybird still on the ivy, it and I, happy to be alive. What beauty we have around us and how often we miss it, in our obsession to achieve goals. I made a mental note, to allow myself more time to exist in my natural state of individualism, whilst appreciating the beauty of my surroundings.

So Tai Chi has saved my sanity again. What a blessing my practise has been over the years, and continues to be to me. I strive to pass on the benefits of Tai Chi and its gifts, to anyone who has the tenacity to endure beyond the superficial. The few, who will dig deep, bare their souls to the universal spirit and practise on a regular basis. The only recipe for true knowledge, that matures into wisdom.

Later that day, I walked the short distance to the cliff top and allowed myself to enjoy the view. Silently giving thanks for my health, the beauty before me and the gift of Tai Chi. So many times, Tai Chi has helped me deal with life's adversities, restored my balance.

How can I show people the value of sustained practise, of this unique and fascinating art? Well, I continue the work, as best I can. For having been introduced to this amazing art, by my Master Chee Soo, given so much from the practice of Tai Chi Chuan, it would be selfish beyond measure not to pass it on to others.

~~~

Is That Mountain High Enough?

Is Tai Chi a hill to climb where effort, struggle and hardships are necessary to reach the pinnacle of attainment?

Or is it a journey of discovery, where every now and then you pause to look and reflect on your achievements so far?

Like most things in Tai Chi, the answer is not straight forward. But perhaps a little story from my own experience will be helpful.

Some time ago I went to the Lake District, to Keswick actually. Whilst enjoying the view near the lake, I turned round and looked at the hill behind me. I pondered on how much better the view would be if I was on top of that hill, looking at the view from that vantage point. So enthused did I become that I felt compelled to climb it to see. So off I went, and being a hot and windless day I was soon sweating and out of breath. But I had started and was not about to give up.

Eventually I reached the top and turned to see my prize, the view. And I was not disappointed, it was magnificent. Sitting on a rock, I relaxed and gazed at the scenery in total wonderment at the beauty and diversity of our wonderful world.

Some time passed, how much I will never know. For at such times, as the beholder of such splendour, I find time somehow becomes obsolete. On days such as these, whilst enjoying a little rest and relaxation, I like to leave my watch behind so as not to be influenced by it. Seeing that the sun was getting lower in the sky and aware that perhaps I should be moving on, I glanced backwards and was surprised to see another hill bigger than the one I had just climbed. The sight of this had been unavailable to me, from my original vantage point down by the lake. I pondered again what the view from this one would look like. Oh! What the heck. Off I went to climb this one too, soon dripping with sweat again and panting heavily.

As I reached the top, in the distance I saw yet another hill, again higher than the one I had just climbed. As I stared at this sight for a minute or so I felt irritated, was there no end to this struggle to reach the best position. My wish to arrive at this place, to see what others who shunned the effort could not. All this effort, my struggle, had yielded nothing more than the knowledge that there is more, always more, requiring more movement, more endeavour necessary to reach a higher understanding.

In my disappointment I turned and was again struck, almost violently, with the magnificence of the vision before me. This achievement had rewarded me with a prize that even surpassed my previous view, the result of that first effort from the foot of the hill near the lake. Had I chosen to stop there, the beauty this standpoint offered, would have been hidden from me.

So I sat there basking in that glorious spectacle. The sun was shining down on me from the beautiful blue sky above, as I enjoyed my prized view, and I suddenly realised the commonality of this experience to my training in Tai Chi. At the outset of my training in Tai Chi I had no idea of the multitude of benefits I would receive. My health and general wellbeing had improved in leaps and bounds.

I remembered a conversation with a fellow Tai Chi practitioner, who had many more years to his credit than I, during my very first advanced training day in Dunstable near London way back in 1976. I had been practising Tai Chi for three years and this was my first day training at the special class held by my Master, Chee Soo for his personally invited students, a real honour. He recognised my enthusiasm and gave me some advice. He told me that this was a special art and it would take me around 15 years before I would be proficient. On my way home back to Yorkshire, at the end of the training day I was rather depressed. 15 years before I would be any good, a lifetime or so it seemed at that time. Fortunately for me, I continued with my studies and I have been rewarded beyond my expectations.

Before setting out on my journey, I could have never known what benefits laid ahead. Nothing from my previous experience could have hinted at the brilliance it would add to my life. Like no one could have described the revelation I now gazed upon, the direct experience had no comparison. Feeling a part of nature, the feeling of being in tune with the world, feeling I was in the right place, following my personal path.

Was the effort worth it, oh, yes! Was I pleased I had made that effort, oh, yes. Did its majesty enthral me, OH! YES!! Am I talking about the view from the hill or the benefits of Tai Chi? Both!

I do my best to enthusiastically encourage others, to make the effort to experience this beauty I have found in my life. But only they can make the journey. They need to want to know more. To make the effort to arrive at this place, this panoramic view that is laid bare before me, my reward. Its splendour can only be discussed with others who have made this or similar journeys themselves. Tai Chi is not a goal to be attained but a never ending journey to be experienced, and that experience will enhance the lives of all those who practice it.

~~~

A Thousand Mile Journey

Progress in our arts can at first be made using reason, to make a structure the mind can fathom with ease. Then as more progress is made, new information and experiences appear, which this structure does not explain. Of course this is a stepping off point for many students, who have gained physical benefit from their practise, but who cannot cope with the paradox presented before them.

Some, those that are ready and willing to, broach this paradox with an open (childlike) mind and keep to the path. These students move into unknown territory i.e. no past experience to link this new, but undeniable experience to.

And here the teacher, the passer on of the depth that he must confer to future generations, has a problem. How to allow the majority of students to enjoy the various physical benefits of the arts. Whilst seeking out those, with the dedication to take on the greater task of learning the deeper aspects of the art, to take them forward, so they do not die within this generation he lives in.

He has a burden he bears sometimes with a heavy heart, but for the most part he experiences a joy unknown to most others. To have such work is a privilege, an honour, and one that requires a commitment to the path, that path often travelling against the crowd. In the process he sometimes gets buffeted and bruised as he drives forward, persistent in his knowledge of the importance of his task. He has a target to hit, not with each shot taken, but by committing himself to keep practising his art like the master archer, until hitting the target gets easier, as his skill increases. An archer learns by doing, picking up the bow and slotting the arrow in place then drawing the bow and with a focused aim sends the arrow on its path.

'A thousand mile journey starts with the first step'

And as he himself continues to learn, he learns that relaxation is the key to his success. No need to run around expounding his abilities to all and sundry. Best leave that to others. Like his practise in meditation has taught him to quieten the mind, empty the glass. For a mind that is full can receive no more learning and nothing can be put in a full glass. We must all empty our lungs to make room for more life giving breath.

As soon as this realization was born in his mind, he remembers one of the last statements his own master spoke to him.

'Let people come to you'

Oh! So long to understand such a simple sentence, I am humbled yet again. So ill prepared for my task yet, I believe I have the courage and determination, and should I fail it will not be for want of trying. Like the man in charge in the control room (whose name no one remembers) when Apollo 13 developed a potentially fatal fault, stated on that fateful but triumphant day.

'Failure is not an option'

~~~

The Supreme Ultimate

T'ai Chi Ch'uan - means 'Supreme Ultimate Fist' but is most often simply referred to as T'ai Chi (Supreme Ultimate). As by far the greatest number of people who learn T'ai Chi nowadays do so for the health benefits rather than for its martial arts aspects.

T'ai Chi conjures up images of hundreds of elderly Chinese, practicing slow and flowing movements in unison. In fact it is practised to such an extent that, in the past, it has drawn the bewildered attention of tourists. All over China many families rise early to complete their T'ai Chi movements in the park, on the rooftops, in car parks and on balconies. In fact anywhere they can find a bit of space, before they go off to work or carry on with the rest of the day. It is not just the slow practice that seems so mysterious to most Westerners, but also the complete lack of self-consciousness of the practitioners, who seem oblivious to being watched and scrutinized in public.

All T'ai Chi students in the west owe their thanks to those masters who brought their family tradition to us, so that we may also enjoy the benefits. And, as with most traditional disciplines, different concepts and ideas become fashionable in later years, which often have little to do with the original facts. So let's take a look at some common myths:

Myth 1: T'ai Chi is only for the elderly.

This is incorrect, T'ai Chi should be taught from an early age, as the art has always been passed from generation to generation, taught to the children almost as soon as they could walk. It is, however, such a safe exercise system that even the elderly benefit, which is why it is so popular amongst the older age group. Balance, the circulation within the various body systems and breathing all improve with practice. Which makes T'ai Chi perfect for those who suffer from stress or the effects of poor posture, for those with joint problems or for those recuperating from illness. For the perfectly healthy, it is an ideal exercise, to make sure they stay that way!

Myth 2: There are only two or three true, original styles.

As anyone who has ever lived in China will tell you, there are many, many different T'ai Chi styles, which were passed on as family traditions over hundreds, and thousands of years – a bit like 'Grandmother's best recipe'. So it is not surprising that all are a little different, some longer than others, some more theatrical than others, some more obvious as a martial art. While in China the various styles are practised next to each other in the parks, in the West there are some T'ai Chi schools which proclaim that their style is 'best', which of course is nonsense. At present, in England, mainly the Yang Style, the Chen Style, the Wu Style and the Lee Style (which we practise), is taught.

Myth 3: T'ai Chi is a martial art only.

It is true that T'ai Chi movements were originally developed as extremely effective, precise, yet flowing self-defence movements. Which made good posture, balance, sure footing, breath-control, and self-control over one's emotions necessary. These are precisely the requisites that make T'ai Chi so useful as a health art and as an art of self-development – the complex movements must be carried out accurately, learned patiently, the slow balance and correct breathing continuously practised.

The self-defence side of the Lee Family Style (called 'Feng Shou', 'Hands of the Wind Style Kung Fu') is taught separately in our classes. This allows people to make their own choice.

Most find T'ai Chi Ch'uan as a health art particularly helpful and therefore it is the majority that practise this side of the art. Some years ago, when Bruce Lee came to fame in the cinema, it was the other way round. T'ai Chi is an important part of both oriental medicine and philosophy, as it helps balance personal energy and aids spiritual awareness. At its most basic level T'ai Chi is excellent for reducing mental stress, and also for reducing tension in the muscles of the body.

Who can benefit from personal T'ai Chi practice?

The answer is just about everyone can improve their general health and well-being with T'ai Chi. Regular practice reduces stress levels, relaxes the body, develops dynamic mind control and promotes good health.

Unlike physiotherapy, T'ai Chi should not be used to fix specific health problems. Instead, it treats the whole person on a continual basis, so that each individual can regain lost vitality or movement due to their whole system working more efficiently. T'ai Chi is the perfect tool to help towards lifelong good health.

As an analogy, lets say you needed to push a lorry. You might need a lot of help to get it rolling, however, once the lorry is moving smoothly little energy is required to keep the momentum going. Your health is the same, if an obstruction occurs you may need lots of help to move it, but, once good health returns only a little regular attention is needed to keep it there.

Health is not the same as fitness, as you can be very fit but still unhealthy, and you can be healthy but not necessarily extremely fit. Again balance is the key. This is where T'ai Chi leaves other forms of exercise way behind and why it is becoming more and more popular, and equally, why more and more people in the medical profession are sending their patients to T'ai Chi classes.

A couple of days ago, Gisela and I were asked to give a talk and demonstration to a gathering of thirty occupational therapists. They felt they needed to know at least a little about T'ai Chi, so they could recommend it to their patients when appropriate, as post treatment exercise. The group as a whole was extremely attentive and every one of them had a go at the T'ai Chi form, a few breathing exercises and some K'ai Men (Chinese Yoga/Chi Gung). At the beginning of the year, I was asked to give a presentation in York at a seminar entitled 'Health at Work in the NHS'. Which again shows that the value of T'ai Chi is appreciated, not only in the alternative health world, but by anyone with their own or their patients' well-being at heart. T'ai Chi burns lots of calories. It improves balance and coordination, more than the best balance training to be found elsewhere. There is no other exercise that can do for you physically what T'ai Chi will.

T'ai Chi is a low impact exercise. The slow movements and your attention to the practice, means you can feel when you are putting undue strain on joints and muscles, so you know when enough is enough - unlike fast and high impact exercise, when injury is only recognized after the event has taken place.

T'ai Chi doesn't leave you dripping with sweat – if it does you are moving too fast. (Trust me, I am a T'ai Chi teacher.) You can practice T'ai Chi in your tea break or any other suitable time, 15 minutes will refresh your mind and rebalance your body. You can practise in your work clothes, in your pyjamas or when and wherever you like - just give yourself a little time and space, to get back in tune with your body - the mind and spirit connection will follow.

Practising T'ai Chi at the start of the day, will focus your mind and relax your body, and that will stay with you in diminishing degrees depending on your encounters throughout your day. Therefore each new day should mean a new time of practice, after all, you cannot keep eating from the same loaf - it will not last forever, and it will get staler and harder as the days go by.

The regular health maintenance and renewed sense of well-being is what keeps those who stick with T'ai Chi enthusiastic - there is a lot more to it all, than just learning some movements by heart.

As Lao Tzu said: "Dealing with things while they are small is easy"- health care is no exception. To feel really well a healthy diet, proper sleep and fulfilling relationships at work and at home are essential. Somehow your T'ai Chi practice will encourage you to look for those things that are good for you, and leave negative situations and habits behind.

Learning T'ai Chi means you throw away tensions and unnecessary movement. You keep simplifying and going back to your essential self – your original self, if you prefer. Forward movement is a product of the mind - necessary of course as the mind is a part of our whole being – racing to accomplish this and that. T'ai Chi redresses the balance by composing and calming the mind whilst relaxing and rejuvenating the body. Coupled with a healthy diet and proper sleep it will assure sound vitality.

Science tells us that we are constantly renewing cells, nearly all of the body is replaced every 5 –7 years. Some cells are renewed every minute of the day.

So change within the body and without is inevitable. We must never fight it, but embrace the developments around us. Life is change. Dance along with the flow while keeping an eye out for obstructions – you don't have to hit them head on, but you can if you insist! The Tao gives you free will, use it wisely. The appreciation of the natural flow of ups and downs and adaptability is something we all need to learn over and over again.

'You are a child of the universe. You have a right to be here.' Just being in the present, experiencing the pure joy of life, is the greatest gift.

T'ai Chi will help you unravel the wonders of life - enjoy!

~~~

The Long Winding Road

The Long Winding Road - That Lead Me To The Starting Line. I started my martial arts training under Steve Babbs an accomplished 'Lao Gar' martial artist. Then one day my training partner came to class, with excited talk of another Kung Fu class in the area. So along we went the next week to check it out. This system seemed to incorporate many more training regimes and we decided to give it a go as well. My pal choose to stop going to the Lao Gar class, but I continued to attend for another few months, before I realised the techniques being taught were vastly different from each other. At least I was finding it confusing and hard to put the two together. So I opted to continue with the new system. They had two nights training a week anyway, so I was a happy bunny. The Lau Gar class only had one session a week.

I had been given some combat training in the Army, which I and my mates referred to as self-defence. I laugh now at the pictures in my mind of those training sessions. Dispensing of 'the enemy' after having sneaked up on them or lay in wait and then attacked, with as much ferocity and single minded intent as we could muster. To subdue them or snuff the life out of them as quickly as possible hardly sounds like self-defence now does it - now does it? Think about this for a moment because I have seen many students of the martial arts over the years who come along to class with this objective in mind, often clouded under the term 'I want to learn self-defence'.

Anyway back to the plot before I drift off and start recalling my old army day's, because my life was about to change big time, forever. I had no idea this change was on its way, I was completely oblivious to it. Some six months later I attended a course taken by Master Chee Soo, who came up to Hull from

London. This first meeting with Chee Soo in 1973 completely fired my imagination. As I watched him training with accomplished martial artists, fascinated by his fluid movements and he seemed so light on his feet, yet his training partners were constantly wrong footed and made to look awkward. I was spell bound. These were not newbie's like me but seriously experienced scrapper's. What I saw that day held me for the next fifteen or so years until I learnt, what I saw was an illusion.

It was real enough but my perception of what I had seen was the illusion. I had been chasing shadows. It wasn't about gaining power over my fellow man but clearing out the dross from my own soul. That was the day I stopped trying to be a better fighter and turned my attention inward and started working on becoming a better me. At long last I knew it was about self development. Then right at that moment a statement Chee Soo made to me after I had been training under him for about 3 years came to me.

One day outside my home as he dropped off some training suits for some of my students he closed the boot of his car and asked me a question. He said 'Do you know why I have been practising the arts for so many years? I was an intelligent student, so I stared at him blankly.

Wow! My brain was in overdrive. Secret knowledge is going to be imparted to me this day, I thought. He continued 'The reason is you are learning about yourself'. He paused and stared into my blank eyes. He went on "No one else, just yourself'. Then he got in his car and drove away, waving a good bye. I think I remember a little twinkle in his eye but I cannot really be sure because I was thinking what the *&^^%$#@! is that supposed to mean.

And there you have it 'When the Student is ready, the Master will appear. He doesn't have to understand, he just has to know he is in the right place at the right time. After all, if I had understood straight away, there would have been no reason to spend the next 21 years studying. And trying to understand that and the many other simple but profound statements Chee Soo made to me and others, over the time I was privileged to train under his guidance.

I have been practising and teaching the arts I learnt under Chee Soo, mostly in the North East of England, since 1976. I am passionate about the unique style and always ready to share my knowledge. For anyone interested in taking a look at our style, I would love to give you a free book of the first five sets (20 Moves) and a video link of myself and my wife practising those moves on the stunning coastline in Scarborough North Yorkshire near their home. It is available to download, so you need an email address to have it sent to you. Go to: www.freetaichibook.co.uk

~~~

Are You Inside Out or Outside In?

Are You Inside out or Outside in? A strange question but let try me to explain myself.

When I first started training in the arts I remember watching the other students and teachers and endeavouring to copy their moves. I wished to draw that fluidity and beauty of movement I saw, into my own Feng Shou and later when I took it up the art of T'ai Chi.

This is of course where we all start out. We see something we aspire to and set out to draw it to us. As we progress we often become irritated as we struggle to get to grips with this now fast becoming mysterious art. We are helped to learn the moves by an already hopefully accomplished practitioner of the arts. Someone who has trod the path before us, and persevered until mastery of those moves was reached. Then grateful for the benefits gained, they choose to give of themselves to share with it others.

When we embark on the study of T'ai Chi, there is no way at the outset, that we would understand that what we see before us is an illusion. We see the form performed before us and that is proof enough. We want what we see. We want T'ai Chi to be ours. We don't understand that T'ai Chi can never become a possession, in the same way that a piece of land or a stretch of water can never be possessed by us. Sure we can buy a stretch of land with a river on it or buy a house by the sea. But that land moves and changes with the years, that water flows, that tide comes in and goes out again. We own an illusion. What we really own is the ability to enjoy that piece of land, that stretch of water, appreciate that view out to sea. We can study it, watch its changing moods and learn to flow with the movement of life as nature does. This is the real value in the practise of T'ai Chi.

T'ai Chi has many drills that require working with a partner. This often puts people off. Someone else invading their space is seen as an intruder and this makes us feel uncomfortable, and out pops our nature, we flee or fight.

T'ai Chi was not called 'The Supreme Ultimate' for no better reason than, it sounded good.

T'ai Chi has the ability to create personal well being for its practitioner. This happens on a physical, mental and energy level, simultaneously. It is also a first class self-defence system.

This balance of the outer activity with the inner feelings and sensations draws the whole person together. Increasing wellbeing, creating a happier person, better equipped to deal with life's up and downs without undue strain.

Focusing only on outer things, clouds our minds to the benefits of inner contemplation. Learning to quiet the mind, not stop it, just to bring it under control. The mind is designed to think and this ability puts us at the top of the animal kingdom. We don't want to stop thinking. We want to do more of it, but real thinking. Not the kind the mind is commonly allowed to be used for. i.e. looking at things that others have done and worrying about things that we have no control over.

T'ai Chi can show you how to use your mind in a more positive way. To put you in control of your life, WOW! wouldn't that be good. Is it worth some effort, you better believe it. Animals have little choice and work mostly on instinct. We can use the mind to take charge of our actions. But as with most things it requires some training first, results come later.

T'ai Chi can show you how to control your body, energy and mental capabilities to a level you have never experienced before. This develops in its wake tranquillity and a sense of happiness that is not experienced by most people, ever.

For most people the mind chatters away and blinds them to the real values and pleasures in life. Conned by the media into fearing this and that catastrophe, which may happen at any moment. Encouraged to acquire more and more possessions, more and more modern machinery to enable us to accomplish more and more in a shorter time frame.

And yet have we gained more time to ourselves, more time to share with our loved ones?

I think most people would answer emphatically, NO!

So these outward possessions bring us little peace. I know only too well how the mind can run away with an idea, and have you rushing around at great speed unaware that you are accomplishing little in the process.

Born under the Sign of Gemini, my brain hits the ground running as I wake. I have learnt to use meditation and T'ai Chi to balance my system. That is probably why I have diligently kept up my practise since 1973. I need it more than most. It is not something I have mastered and can now forget. I need to constantly and consistently practise. Like our muscles, if we don't use them, they atrophy. To get the most benefit, we all must exercise a little to keep in good condition.

Oh Yes! I still practise on a daily basis. There is no end to the practise of T'ai Chi. Its greatest benefits come from within the PRACTISE. The outward physical movements will lead you to your inner self, the real you. Not the one people see, not the one they think you should be.

Why not make up your mind, to use the enormous power available to you through your T'ai Chi practise. To draw this power into you, to expand your life in a positive way. Find the jewel and polish it until it becomes a thing of beauty, admired by all who see it. But don't do it for others, don't do it to show off. Do it for the best of all reasons; do it for yourself.

But be warned the process deals some painful blows. As you strip away the layers, and dig deep to seek the jewel within, you will meet obstacles, you will be tempted to quit. Take the easier road; jump back on the bandwagon, join the rat race again.

If you can persevere with your practise, and you can if you want, it only requires a decision to do so on your part. You will be rewarded with a life that is mostly full of good health, enthusiasm for your work, a real possession in these times of change in the world.

You see T'ai Chi teaches you that toughness is not an external thing, it is internal. Born of years of dedicating oneself to the task, perseverance is a dirty word to most these days. We are encouraged to go for the quick solution. But houses that withstand the storms are build on good foundations. Good foundations take time to build.

Don't fear the future; no doubt the world is unfolding as it should. Don't look out and complain about what you see. Look inward and work on yourself. After all, the only person you can control without using force is yourself.

T'ai Chi can help you bring yourself under control, and if you persist with your practise keep you there and better it, again and again. There is no limit; the only limit is one you impose on yourself.

Set yourself free with your practise of T'ai Chi – The Supreme

Ultimate.

The best exercise for the whole person there is – bar none

Quote from a legend in his own lifetime

'I know where I'm going and I know the truth and I don't have to be what you want me to be. I'm free to be what I want'.
Muhammad Ali

~~~

Tai Chi - To Be or Not To Be

One of the problems experienced by new students to Tai Chi is they often complain they cannot remember the moves. Because Tai Chi relaxes the body and dulls the thought processes, the moves are often easily forgotten but the essential benefits of Tai Chi i.e. the meditative experience is remembered. Because it is absorbed into their being.

This is the beauty of Tai Chi for the newcomer. The inner experience outweighs the outer, and as this is an unfamiliar experience, the mind fights it. Because it does not understand and cannot define the experience by looking at other experiences. The mind wants to understand, to link to a past experience and to commit that experience to memory. Now we have a big problem. The new student feels good after the class, but when trying to relate their experience to others, finds it difficult to put it into words what that experience was. Because essentially it was an experience that was felt, not deciphered by the mind.

Tai Chi practice should refresh you; not burden you with more things to remember. True understanding in Tai Chi brings a deep wholeness to your essential being. Not another memory attached to the intellect. There is no need to remember it – it is there…

As you practise let thoughts come and let them pass through. Become the watcher. Be indifferent to the thoughts. When you listen or read words of wisdom, don't try to remember them or the meaning will be lost. Let them wash over you, cleaning your mind, emptying it. Do not let thoughts whip up your mind like a strong wind, ruffling the surface, causing confusion and doubt, be still like a calm lake. The purpose of meditation is to throw out the mind. Tai Chi empties the mind. Do not burden yourself with more words or thought processes.

See from your deep inner self, let that wisdom go to work to change and empower your essential self, the real inner you. Forget for the moment your outer self, your conscious self that was born of your upbringing, your surroundings and moulded by others' expectation of you and what you should become.

Tai Chi given the chance can change your life, if you let it. This is true, I know beyond a shadow of doubt because I am living proof of that.

Being of service to others, by passing on the teaching I was so privileged to receive from my Tai Chi Master and spiritual mentor. I am living a life of happiness and satisfaction beyond my wildest dreams. I have found my personal Dao.

Perhaps I was lucky, but I really believe I had the sense to see the Master when I met him and intuitively felt that this was what I should be doing. I didn't understand why, it just felt right and I did not deny that or subdue it with logic. I followed my heart though the good and the bad times and allowed my inner self to flower.

~~~

Don't Forget to Enjoy The View!

There I was at the crack of dawn (9.30am actually) too dark at
6.30am at least that was my reasoning for doing my T'ai Chi
practise mid morning. As is often the case I decided to do a
Dao Yin exercise first, today I choose 'Wave the Hands' a
personal favourite of mine.

The day was extremely windy, but in the confines of my garden
not so bad as to disrupt my T'ai Chi practise. As I raised my
hands over my head and looked skyward I couldn't help
noticing how some small clouds were flying along on the wind.
Quite low and pushed along at great speed by the rushing air
current. Then I noticed how the bigger yet more spread out
clouds, which were much higher, appeared motionless. And of
course I then just had to go inside for pen and notebook to
record the thought.

The resemblance of all in nature to our development in our
unique arts, and how very, very fortunate I was. To have been
able to train under Chee Soo's supervision and learn so many
fascinating things about myself and the world around me, that
were hitherto beyond my comprehension.

I told Gisela of my thoughts later that day after my T'ai Chi
practise, and we had an interesting conversation about the
similarities between the clouds behaviour and learning sticky
hands (I Fu Shou).

How when we are new to the art, we dart about physically and
mentally, just like the young clouds being rushed around by the
air currents. Then as we learn, how much more like the older
higher clouds we become. Observing the events below and
around us, we move less but achieve more. Less investment in
energy expenditure and less disruption to our immediate

surroundings. Learning to move with the flow, rather than trying to move forward too forcefully. Enjoying and interacting with the experience, for after all this is life, is it not, moment to moment in the present.

I am reminded of this beautiful saying by an unknown author I have framed and hung above my desk:

Take Time To See

It seems so hard to understand, as I look out across the land, that all I view belongs to me, I ought to take more time to see.

The distant hills and mountains high, the rolling clouds and bright blue sky, no one can take these views from me, as long as I have eyes to see.

A timid deer with a haunting look, who stands refreshed by yonder brook, knows not that he belongs to me, oh, what a thrilling sight to see!

The song of birds so gay and clear, that fill the morning air with cheer, and fragrant flowers of every hue, That stand erect bedecked with dew; all these and more belong to me. If I but use my eyes to see.

When evening shadows gather night, and twinkling stars light up the sky, I hear my Master say to me, "I made it all for you to see!"

My heart grows warm with faith and pride, To know that He is by my side.

Set yourself free with your practise of T'ai Chi.

The Supreme Ultimate.

The best exercise for the whole person there is – bar none.

~~~

I Fu Shou

(Sticky hand/Adhering hand)

The object of the I Fu Shou exercise is to upset your partner's balance. This is not because it is a competition with a winner and a loser. Although sadly I see that 'pushing Hands competitions' are starting to appear. With some T'ai Chi Organizations subsequently advertising that one of their students won this or that section, presumably in the belief that this will attract more students to their organization.

The types of students that this attracts, are the ones who want to win competitions and show off in front of a crowd. I feel this is a retrograde step that moves away from the true spirit of T'ai Chi. I do not consider that I Fu Shou should be presented as a form of competition, which inevitably breeds a winner and a loser. I consider it to be a voyage of self-discovery. The practice of which, will enable the practitioner to develop a heightened state of awareness. Firstly of themselves, then others they come into contact with. There is nothing to lose but your ego. And the prize to be won, is humility.

Perhaps by looking at the names given to parts of this exercise we can understand the different philosophy behind them. Firstly, to push, this word is defined as meaning: to exert force on a thing, to move away from oneself or from the origin of the force. This in essence seems rather an aggressive attitude.

This type of philosophy leads to ambition, desire, and glorification of the self and the wish to make oneself superior. This inevitably leads to separation from the Tao (way). There is no harmony here; only conflict. 'Sticky' is defined as tending or intended to stick or adhere. Adhere is defined as: stick fast to a surface, another substance, etc. Also, to behave according to, follow in detail or give support or allegiance. These words explain the essence of the instruction I received from my master. He always taught me that once contact has been made it must be maintained, and that this contact should be light, so light in fact, that if a feather where to fall upon your arm it would sink under the weight of the feather. He also taught me that the object of the exercise was to follow the movements of your partner. Not to force them to change the direction, but to allow them to move their hand and arm in whatever way they wish. Learning to work within this framework whilst maintaining your own balance, giving in to their force, which completely negates their strength and allows you to gently guide them in the direction they wish to go. Gently, helping them on their way.

If you offer no resistance, then no matter how much force is used against you, it cannot restrict your freedom. By giving in to that force and offering no resistance, your partner sacrifices their balance when they exert force against your arm. By this action they create a weakness within their posture that can be exploited, allowing you to maintain your balance whilst upsetting theirs. The object of this is not to gain power over your partner, but to learn to remain in control of your own balance, whilst being put under pressure by your partner. This helps us to deal with the problems we encounter in everyday life, without losing control and resorting to violence. And by violence I do not necessarily mean physical violence but also mental violence, which is the modern way to bully and make people fear you. Power hungry people weave their webs of mental manipulation, praying on the weak within our society - we are all weak at some time or another as we fall into our yin periods during our journey through life.

There are no laws, that can be enforced effectively, that will eradicate this kind of mental violence that we all have to suffer at some time or other at work, from parents, teachers and countless enthusiastic exponents of officialdom. We just have to learn to deal with it. We have to learn to take responsibility for ourselves. Instead of becoming physically or verbally violent which can only escalate the conflict, we have to learn to absorb the energy thrown our way.

In doing so we strengthen ourselves and weaken the perpetrator, but more importantly we remain entire.

~~~

Resistance Is Futile

As a student and teacher of Tai Chi since 1973, one of the greatest benefits to my general health and well being has been to learn that resistance is futile. In the sense of trying to overcome a force, either physically or mentally greater than yourself. Because it inevitable leads to injury, physically or mentally.

When something or somebody resists you, the wise yield, while others resist/fight.

The resistance you are encountering is not for you, it is a condition suffered by the other person or thing blocking your present path. The fact that you are in its path is just a coincidence. It is just something passing through, a temporary situation or state. Do not take it personally. See it as it is, something outside of you.

Don't let it in, if you do it will infiltrate and destroy, eat away at your inner being, consume your mind. Keep it where it belongs outside, separate.

See it as you would see the rainy day when you wished to go walking or play tennis or some other outdoor activity.

Distinguish it as merely an irritation, which can be dealt with by taking control of your mind and then finding another exciting indoor activity to do instead.

You have this power within you. You are the controller of your destiny, but only if you believe it, and only if you use it.

Life is often like a storm arriving, an unfathomable natural condition of forces beyond your control. Let it pass. If you resist it will build in power and cause much damage. If you can let it pass through, the disturbance will be minimal. And when harmony returns, you will be unscathed and able to move on towards your dreams and goals.

The story of King Canute is usually misrepresented as an example of the King's arrogance. The truth is that King Canute set his throne by the sea shore and commanded the tide to halt and not wet his feet and robes. The King wanted to show his people that even though he was a King, he was powerless before nature and God.

The King continued to command the tide to halt. However, the tide continued to rise and washed over his feet and legs without respect to his royalty.

Then the king moved backwards, turning to the watching crowd and said: "Let all men know, empty and worthless is the power of kings, for there is none worthy of the name, but He whom heaven, earth, and sea obey by eternal laws." He then hung his gold crown on a crucifix, and never wore it again "to the honour of God the almighty King", the ruler of all nature. It is a shame that his actions have been distorted, for the true story imparts much wisdom.

If you fight the storm when it enters your life, you will probably sustain mid to severe damage or worse as a result. And when the disturbance passes, waste much time returning your life to its position before the calamity hit.

Day to day minor and occasionally major aggravations infiltrate our lives at work, within our families and through our own belief systems.

How we react to those disturbances affects the quality of life we experience.

~~~

Reflections

As I walk along the harbour, I pause for a while to rest on one
of the many vacant seats. Sitting there looking out across the
bay, I enjoy the quiet and solitude. The light from the street
lamps is reflected in the water. And as the water ripples,
disturbed by the cold evening breeze, the spot of light that is
the reflection of the bulb in the street lamp is duplicated on
each ripple. The ripples stretch away from the harbour wall,
towards the wharf where the boats are moored. Here the water
is less affected by the wind and the ripples fade away and with
them the lamps reflection fades too. I look up at the lamps in
the street and then down at the reflections stretching away
from the harbour wall. The water disturbed by the wind creates
ripples and these ripples reflect the light from the lamp. When
the water is calm it will only reflect a single light, a near perfect
replica of the original. Yet when the water is disturbed it
reflects many more lights, and the more reflections there are
the more distorted they become.

We are like this, disturbed by the winds of existence we are
rippled and become a many faceted reflection of the shining
light that is the supreme spirit. Like the distorted reflections of
the street lamp I gaze upon we become distorted too. Instead
of being a unique replica of the one real light and radiating that
true light in our own individual way. We allow the winds of life
to disturb our naturally calm interior. We become ruffled, we
lose our equilibrium, we become confused and lose our way,
becoming disconnected from our own personal Tao.

It is late evening and there are only a few people about. I
reflect on the changing scene, the movement from summer to
autumn has produced a metamorphosis to the area. A few
short weeks ago the harbour, beach and streets were teeming

41

with holiday makers. Some walked along like me, enjoying the scenery, some walked hand in hand with lovers, husband or wife sometimes followed by children. Some filtered into the amusements, pubs and clubs, seeking entertainment. I wondered how anyone could come to such a beautiful place and then spend all their time in a pub drinking. Presumably they do it in an effort to escape from the unpleasant boring existence which they have to endure the rest of the year. How anyone could feverishly play bingo for hour after hour, blind to the natural beauty all around, preferring the material gain which is theirs, when they complete that magic line or fill up those four corners on their card. Eager just to take back home more than they came with, a modern measure of success; the acquisition of material possessions. All this I find hard to understand, to me it seems like some self-inflicted torture.

As I sit reflecting on these things, I remember that I have done all those things and more. I have no right to judge, I do not know who these people are and their struggle with the daily toil of existence may well be fraught with more difficulties than I encounter. They must travel their path and I must travel mine. I have made a conscious effort to change my life. Perhaps these people do not realise they have a choice. Caught in the stream of life, they move with whoever seems to know what to do and where to go. The one who battles hardest against the flow. And in the process makes the most disturbance, is the most easily seen. So they get lost in the struggle to emulate this prominent apparently successful example. Blinded by fear, fear of being different, fear of the unknown, fear of failure in a world ruled by material values. Full of fear they huddle together like sheep, for there is safety in numbers, so they say. But huddled together with most of their movement dictated by the group, this stifles individual development, restricts their individual freedom. To always be looking outwards to what you want to be, to where you want to go, to be always searching for more material growth to satisfy the modern view of what a successful person should be like, in this there is no personal freedom, no personal happiness.

To have the courage to look within to see who you are, to learn to know yourself, this I believe is the way to personal happiness and freedom. When you know who you are, THEN you know the way forwards. This knowledge can, I believe, only be reached by searching within. If you do not know who you are, how can you possibly come to know your own personal path (Tao). Trying to be what others would have us become, is of no use. If we listen to others who believe they know what is best for us and then follow that advice blindly, this is surely foolish and places us in the same realm as automated machines and robots. Once we follow this path our actions become mechanical, predictable and no longer able to cope with the ever changing conditions that life puts before us. Reality is chaos and needs spontaneous action, not mechanical reactions.

When the sea is rough, it stirs up the sand near the shore. Disturbed water in a pond, brings the mud to the surface. A ruffled mind raises sediment to the surface and all manner of calamities follow. Looking at nature is one way I find useful to calm the mind, which allows the sediment to sink, so that my thoughts are purified again. Looking at the hills, mountains, lakes, rivers, sea and open skies, one can learn to put one's own troubles in perspective. For in the great scheme of things they do not amount to much. But in the great scheme of things YOU count for a lot, everything in fact. The most important person in your life is YOU. The more you come to know your true self, who you really are, where you come from, the better balanced you will become. A pure reflection of the shining light. Your mind will become more tranquil and serenity will follow. But this act of gaining self knowledge can only be initiated by you, following someone else because they have a lifestyle that seems good or a disposition you think you would like to have too will not do it. A conscious effort on your part to be still, to look and see, to listen and hear what goes on outside of you and how this movement effects you. What emotions, desires and fears does this outward movement raise in you? By looking at yourself in this way whilst remaining calm, refusing to let the momentum on the outside effect your personal equilibrium, if you can train yourself to do this, then the true nature of the situation will become clear to you. If you allow yourself to enter into the situation, you will be affected by the disturbance and lose your clarity. And any action you may take in the light of this will be distorted to the degree that you allowed your clarity to be disrupted.

To learn anything one needs time and patience and of course a good teacher. Through conscious effort the first two can be secured. By exercising self-discipline by consciously setting aside time to accomplish the task, then by patient study, we can set ourselves on the road to knowledge. Our colleges and universities are full of students studying a diverse range of subjects with which to enhance their careers. Finding a teacher for these subjects to acquire knowledge of the external side of life is relatively easy. For those interested in self development in a spiritual sense, finding a teacher with special knowledge, esoteric knowledge, is another matter. Because often those who claim to have this knowledge are charlatans. Who line their pockets with gullible peoples money whilst proclaiming their virtue and offering instant enlightenment, at a price. The genuine Master is not a prominent figure who is easily found, he or she goes about their work without the flashy glib self advertising of the charlatan. True Masters speak in simple terms so that they can be understood by all. They do not need to use complicated language to elevate themselves, their very presence and their natural sincerity ennobles them. When they teach in whatever form that may take, they do just that, they teach. They use simple language and actions to pass on the knowledge that they have been given. This knowledge is there for all to see but is often missed, because most people are unable to see, the profound truths in such humble behaviour, their minds are blinded by the simplicity of it. They prefer to define what they see and hear, prefer to look for complicated structures to analyze, then link the conclusions they reach to similar patterns stored in their memories. Unable to still the mind and just see and hear without introducing their own ideas into the equation, they cast a cloud over what they are being shown that dims their perception of the truth. If you shut out the light, then whether this is intentional or through ignorance it makes no difference, the result is the same; you will be blind.

This I believe is why so many false prophets appear and collect followers so easily. They give people what they want, smart clever phases to repeat, told of what they will experience through the practices they are given, they then set out to accomplish these goals, for most illusions quickly follow. You are in charge of your destiny no one else, only you can find your own path, let no-one else tell you what you are. A true Master will show you how to reach deep within yourself, so you can be your own salvation from the trammel and confusion that surrounds us all during the movement that is our existence. As the Moon (Yin) and Sun (Yang) exert their influence on the sea and cause the tides to disturb the calm waters. So does the Yin and Yang of our own life cause us to lose our equilibrium, clouding our minds in the process.

So learning to still the mind and bring it under your control is of paramount importance, if you wish to learn the inner knowledge. To know who you are, what your path in life is, from where you came and to where you will return. Logic, the man made tool used to define our external material world will have to be dispensed with temporarily, it has no use here. It will only hinder progress. For logic interferes with the truth and tries to categorize things, placing them in compartments with the known, the collection of things learnt from past experiences and stored in memory. These experiences will never be repeated. You may experience similar circumstances, but they will never be exactly the same.

The new is always fresh, the vibrant truth cannot be linked to the past, the past is gone, irretrievable, spent. The future awaits us. But the present is here, right in this very moment, this is where the truth is, in the precious present. And to see it, we must still the mind so we can experience it, see it clearly, just as it is.

The mind to me is like the sea, the surface is easily ruffled by the wind, but the deep waters are more tranquil. The surface of the mind, the part we use in everyday life to deal with the necessities of survival, making a living etc, is easily disturbed. The deeper parts of the mind are rarely used by most people, some say that we use only one tenth of the minds capacity. By taking time to be alone, using that time to shut out everyday influences so that the surface of the mind can be calmed, we can reach the deeper recesses of the mind. Reach the source, become in touch with our true nature unfettered by the external movement of man.

As all artists know, the reflection of colours in water shows the light colours darker and the dark colours lighter. The reflection we see of ourselves in a mirror is not how we look to other people. Therefore to look at our outward reflection and then accept this as the truth is folly. To ask others for an appraisal based on their view, as to how they see us and how they feel about our behaviour, has great value and is useful as feedback as to how others see you. However, this view of you as expressed by others must not be taken to be the whole truth, for it will inevitably be clouded by their own individual perception. The truth, the whole truth requires you to work on yourself, to still the mind to bring it under your conscious control. When you have calmed the waters of your mind and the impurities have sunk, then you will be able to see with a clarity that previously you denied yourself. So be still, look around you and just watch, see the beauty in nature, see also the ruthlessness and violence, but do not focus only on the negative aspect of things. See the evil deeds done by others who seek power over their fellow man and to gain great material riches, see their anger and unhappiness. See the kindness shown to others by some who help their fellow men and find pleasure in doing so without demanding or expecting any excessive reward, see their happy joyous faces. Then look at yourself and see the good and the bad, see the truth. For not until you can see the truth within yourself can you consciously choose, choose to hinder or help, choose to destroy or build, choose to be aggressive or kindly, choose to hate or love.

We cannot always be correct, our behaviour will always be seen by some to be bad no matter how hard we try to be good. The perspective of others and therefore their expectations will not always match ours. Man by his very nature destroys things to live. The food we eat to sustain us, even if we do not eat the flesh of others animals. is produced by violent means. We pick fruits and vegetables, pull the fruit from their trees and bushes, wrench the vegetables out of the ground. We harvest the grains, cut them down so we may live on. However, if we endeavour not to over indulge ourselves and not unnecessarily waste food, there will be more for those who have not enough. If we take only what we need, we will not become obese through over eating; but we must take enough for our needs if we are to develop properly physically and mentally, if we have not enough food we cannot sustain a good quality existence. So to eat too little through fear of getting fat or depriving others less fortunate than ourselves would be foolish. Both extremes produce poor health and deny us the ability to express ourselves fully. Balance is as always the key and as always you must find your own balanced diet.

Improvements, real improvements, are made not by looking at others and then seeing their faults setting about correcting them. This would require us to exert our will upon others which will cause us to become self-righteous and impose our beliefs by force. Whether that force is of a physical nature or mental manipulation or through force of law. I believe real improvement, can only be made when we decide to look within ourselves, and then consciously make an effort to create an improvement within the self. Thereby making an improvement, albeit a small one, to the whole of mankind. The more people that do this, the greater the overall improvement will be. The harmony and kinship that follows will create long term peace and progress, unlike the short term improvement that is the result of coercing others to follow rules and laws dictated to them. For as soon as the force or the fear of punishment is no longer present, its influence swiftly disappears. Amendments and betterment to ourselves will influence humanity as a whole for the good and create a higher existence here on earth. One that can be sustained indefinitely; sustained by our own will. The Tao/God gives us free will to make our own choices, let us use this gift wisely.

~~~

What! - My Laptop Just Did Tai Chi

As I sat there, watching my laptop work away, I was blow away by the similarity, between what I was witnessing and the experiences of a seasoned Tai Chi practitioner...

I had recently ungraded my internet connection, to a wireless one. Something I have wanted to do, for a couple of years now. But whenever I researched, by asking friends and techie types in computer stores, I always received conflicting views, on how stable a wireless, as against a wired connection was.

The wired connection was fine, apart from three points, 1. My artist wife Gisela, could not use the netbook in her studio, 2. I quite fancied using my laptop, in the garden. 3. We had a wire trailing across the top of the stairs, to my office computer, which is in a spare bedroom. Neither of the first two were convenient, and in the case of the wire at the top of the stairs, it was downright doggy, safety wise.

Then along came a well respected friend of the techie brigade, and he assured me, he thought we would be fine. In fact he had recently moved house and changed his ISP for his broadband connection, who had kindly given him another router. This is the hardware, that connects to the phone line and the other computers, without needing wires. He offered to set it up for us, using his old spare router and if we were not happy with it we could simply revert back, to our wired system.

A free trial and easy to revert back to our old system, meaning no risk, I had no problem with that. So along he came a few days later, and said it would take probably half an hour - Yeh right! We are dealing with computers here – So one and half hours later and a telephone call to my ISP for technical assistance, which I must say were excellent, we got connected.

They supplied information we needed that we would never have discovered ourselves. Here is a very important point, about learning the depth of Tai Chi or any other field of study, requiring sustained effort over time. But that should be the topic of another article, as I am in danger of running off the subject of this one.

Over the next day or so, all seemed fine and so I grew in confidence, using this new technology. Gisela took her notebook into her studio, whilst working away on her mosaics and listening to YouTube.

A short time later we had a fine day, and I took my laptop into the garden, to do some work on our monthly newsletter, whilst getting some welcome sun on my face.

Then it hit me my laptop has just done Tai Chi.

You see, I needed a file from my other computer in my upstairs office, and here I was now downloading a file onto my laptop, from my computer upstairs in the house. No Wires, no obvious link between the two computers, and Bob's your uncle, there was the file. No trekking upstairs and sifting through this computer's files, then transferring it to a pen stick (a small storage device making it easy to transfer from one computer to another).

The very thing that separates Tai Chi, from most other forms of exercise, is the way it works on and builds up the energy system of the body. Students new to Tai Chi are usually concerned with improving their physical health and enjoying the relaxing feeling Tai Chi practise brings. Through the regular practise of Tai chi and its sister arts of Kai Men and Dao Yin, the benefits to your health are many and long lasting.

But if they are still around in a few years time

Students usually become fascinated, by the energy side of Tai Chi. Now before you think I am one of those aerie fairy types, who are off their rocker on cloud nine. Let me point out, that science now states that everything is energy. It is just that those solid objects, vibrate at a different level to us and other things. Everything all around us, inside and out, is energy vibrating at different frequencies. Just because we cannot see that does not mean it is not real.

If you care to read a book about the fascinating things that scientists are working on, at the moment. Try the 'Dance of the 'WU LI MASTERS' by Gary Zukav An overview of the new physics, it is one amazing book. Check it out on YouTube where Gary talks about the book. There are many others to choose from 'The Dao of Physics' an Exploration of the Parallels between Modern Physics and Eastern Mysticism, is a book by physicist Fritjof Capra and is another, I found informative and thought provoking.

Al Chung-Liang Huang a Tai Chi Master

Among contributors to the 'Dance of the WU LI Masters' is Al Chung-Liang Huang, a Tai Chi Master. For me, the technical explanations in this book were not always easy reading, but in most areas, things are explained in language that is easily understandable and totally fascinating. I drove my poor students mad for months afterwards, as I linked things from the book to my lessons in Tai Chi, the comparisons were amazing. After studying and teaching Tai Chi since 1973, to me the principles appear in almost everything I learn about everything else. And how could it be not so. Tai Chi is based on the natural laws of the universe and everything in the universe must adhere to these principles also.

When we think - We activate our energy

Energy moves the body

So when we practise Tai Chi, we must first calm the mind, bring it under control and direct it to our purpose. If you haven't got a purpose for learning Tai Chi, it is doubtful you will continue for long. The mind untrained, is like an unruly child. Undisciplined it will run into trouble, sooner rather than later. Controlling the mind is one of Tai Chi's necessary traits and also attributes. So if you haven't got a purpose for your practise, bringing your mind more under your control, may well be a good one for you.

Although your initial purpose does not have to be so lofty an ideal to start with, just wanting to relax more or getting out of the house and meeting other people, is enough to keep you going at the start.

Getting back to the computer. When you want to use it to accomplish a task, you open the required program and start the work. But first you had a thought, a purpose, something you wanted to achieve. Once you have that, you can find the tools i.e. program in this case, to start the work. A computer will not work unless it has energy (electricity). Then driven by your purpose, you can produce an email, edit a photo, create a drawing, write an article and send that out into the world, to where ever you choose. Or print out a hard copy and send it, to whoever you choose to.

Our brain is rather like a computer, it has a memory section (hard drive). The ability to analyse data, with its processor, assisted by its loaded programs. Not unlike our power of reason, that allows us to analyse information, which we pass through our past experiences, to come to a conclusion of the way forward.

Our brain then gives out instructions and our energy mobilizes, to give fuel to our muscles and thought processes, so we can carry out the task at hand. Without energy, none of this is possible.

However, most of us never give this subject any thought, like our breathing, we take it for granted, we assume it is an automatic function of our existence, and it is. But if ,for some reason, we struggle to breathe, or suffer a lack of energy. We soon realise that a lack of either, is very restrictive indeed.

So it would seem to me, to be a good idea to learn a little about our energy systems. Not because we are in short supply now, but to ensure that if, in the future should we become deficient, we will always have a way of ensuring we can build up adequate reserves again.

My teacher, Master Chee Soo used to say when you are born you have a bucket full of chi, when you use it up you die, so don't waste it.

When we are young we think we are indestructible, and often fritter away energy in unhealthy practices and behaviour. As we get older and develop, we learn to conserve our energy and to the extent we do this, we keep our health into old age.

Tai Chi teaches us to relax and conserve our energy, and also how to replenish it, prolonging its life and keeping the quality of our chi good. Like the computer needs electricity to function, we need our chi. The quality and quantity, should be, of great concern to us. Healthy exercise such as Tai Chi, along with breathing exercises and good quality healthy food, can make a vast difference to the quality of life we experience.

There are many forms of exercise available today, but not many that have been around for as long as Tai Chi. Tai Chi survives because is it as perennial, as the earth under our feet. Based on nature itself, a tool for self-development, and in my opinion, Tai Chi is the best health exercise system there is, bar none.

~~~

Reality

In MY house, in My mind, I can meditate and draw within to find the real me. This essence, this seed I can only find in the inner me and this jewel within will tell me who I am, show me my true path in life. To sit in contemplation has its value, but to spend hours each day sitting alone in my house is not life in total. I must venture outside where danger lurks. Outside are all the pleasures and dangers of life.

My reason for staying inside is often safety, I feel in control, in my house that is familiar to me. If someone wishes to enter they must approach the door and knock, I am able to control to a large extent who may gain entry. But outside there are no walls to confine, no doors to limit access. My fear that I will be hurt will sooner or later come true, I will encounter my share of life's difficulties. However, rather than fear these experiences I must learn to embrace them for they are the Yin (negative) aspects of my own existence. Without the Yin there can be no Yang (positive). Whilst this may sound unsavory to our pleasure seeking minds it is never the less true, for can we have day without night, sun without rain, man without woman? Of course not, this is nature's way, opposites oppose each other but they also complement each other. A contradiction in terms perhaps, but we all must accept it for this apparent chaos fuels the fire of life. It is my belief that all the lessons to be learned are there before our very eyes, in nature. Outside, danger lurks, this is undisputed, but outside there is also the opportunity to experience many joys, the chance to give and receive the pleasures of life's bounteous gifts. Inside is limited - yet peace resides here, but death prowls here also. Outside is life in perpetual motion, uncontrollable, many dangers lie concealed here waiting to happen. The Yin and Yang of life.

Nature in her raw magnificently chaotic unpredictable state. Totally beautiful, awesomely majestic. Outside, in the movement of existence we call life, we must learn to adapt to ever changing circumstances, to move with the flow. To understand through experience, its essence, then coupling that understanding with a consideration of our own path, we may progress without resisting the universal Tao(way), and in the process experiencing true freedom without conflict. Learning to be like water ourselves, so that when confronted with an obstacle, we can either wait gathering power until we can flow effortlessly over it, or changing our path find the way of least resistance and flow around it.

Man is inventive by nature, we seem to have an insatiable appetite to create things, but we are only really capable of copying nature, only the Tao (God) can create, we merely copy. For is not an aeroplane a manmade bird. And is not an aquanaut and travel in other underwater craft no more than our attempts to experience life as an aquatic animal. Danger lies hidden in the aeroplane and underwater craft, many are killed and injured making a voyage using these methods of transportation. Does this make their inventors murderers or guilty of mass manslaughter? What of the pleasure gained through using these modes of conveyance, because of the ease of foreign travel they permit, people are intermingling, broadening their personal horizons. The walls of fear are slowly breaking down and we are becoming closer to our brothers and sisters in other countries, sharing our cultures and experiences. So should we honour those responsible for the design of these vehicles of communication and enlightenment? And there we have the Yin and Yang of it, the Yin and Yang of life. Outside lies both danger and pleasure, possible injury and development, death and life. These are inseparable, this is the way (The Tao). Accept it, for you cannot change it, it is the essence of nature.

I was horrified while watching a wildlife programme on television the other day. Cheetahs were running down their quarry and then choking them to death by enclosing the throats of their victim in their jaws. Yet they weed out the weak, sick and old and therefore help in their own way to maintain the health of the herd they prey upon, as only the strong and wily escape their clutches. This programme reminded me of another video I have, part of the series "The Trials Of Life" a natural history series brought to us by Sir David Attenborough. Well known for his unique and enthusiastic portrayal of natural history. Called 'Hunting and Escaping' the programme contained scenes, many of which have never before been captured on film, which fill you at times with indignation and horror. A startling contrast between the beauty and grace of these wonderful creatures; with whom we share the planet and the violence with which they obtain their food. He educates us to the realities of our own survival. We shop at the supermarket for our food but either deliberately or through ignorance; blind ourselves to the process that gets our food on the supermarket shelves.

Using the very latest technology Sir David Attenborough shows us, with dramatic examples, how these animals behave, how they use their bodies, their unique skills to hunt or to escape, and in so doing, survive; to pass on their genes to the next generation. Music is used sparingly in the programme and quite rightly so. For what could be better music for a natural history programme than the natural sounds of the planet: the waves of the sea, the wind, the animals moving through the leaves and trees, the natural sounds of creatures crawling, slithering, through the undergrowth.

The natural sounds create an atmosphere that is as unique as David Attenborough's narration. You almost forget that you are sitting in your own living room at home. At times, as the programme reaches one of its many dramatic climaxes. You feel you are, right there, moving quickly, slightly out of breath, your heart pounding, just behind and eagerly following the enthusiastic David Attenborough.

Wait a minute though! I am a civilized human being, and we are following an animal going 'IN FOR THE KILL'. I am not that sort of person - I do not believe in experiments using animals - I support campaigns to protect endangered species. Granted they are only killing for food to feed themselves. But why am I following the action so enthusiastically? Am I following long forgotten basic survival instincts which are no longer necessary in the modern world, where I can collect my food from the supermarket, after, it has been cleaned and neatly packaged? Would I, stripped of every modern convenience, returned to the wilds where edible vegetation was not enough to support life, kill for food?

Watching "Hunting and Escaping" again made me uncomfortably aware, that although we are living in a modern civilized society, we are all still animals with the same basic instincts. Although most of us do not 'hunt and escape' to survive and find our food anymore, we still hunt and escape in other ways in our daily life. At our place of work we may dodge (escape) the boss when he is in a bad mood. Ask for a raise or promotion (hunt) when we feel we are in a powerful position, when we for instance withdraw essential services which would inconvenience others, or perhaps go on strike to obtain better pay and conditions. Are we not fighting for survival the modern way, trying to ensure a reasonable standard of living for our families, so that we can survive and pass on our genes to the next generation?

David Attenborough's programme investigates the animal kingdom. He studies their behaviour, their habits, their relationship with their habitat and neighbours. He then very subtly and skillfully hints at the analogy between their behaviour and ours, pointing out that the structure of our modern society evolved from these roots. It seems to me we are all animals still. The characters in David Attenborough's beautifully produced programmes, are just more honest about it, than are we so called; Civilized Human Beings'.

~~~

Construction And Destruction

These two opposites are to most peoples way of thinking entirely different conditions, one good and one bad. Can we have construction without destruction? I would give the emphatic answer NO! Because it seems to me this is what nature tells us. All growth in nature starts with a seed or embryo and if nutrition is available develops into a mature specimen of its species. But after a time, without exception, degeneration sets in and retrogression takes a hold of its physical properties, deterioration acts upon the corporeal bodies until they quit the temporal plane of existence. So all life is ephemeral, birth, growth, old age, ending with decline and decay. To provide growth all in nature needs sustenance, something must cease to be so that something else can be nourished and grow. How long any individual organism will survive no one knows.

Cage an animal and you reduce its experience of reality, diminish its quality of life. Confined, denied its natural environment, whether through protective influences or self imposed through fear, is to negate life and reduce it to a zombie like state for sempiternity. What an inconceivable atrocity, what a heinously cruel act.

Yet how many of us cage ourselves willingly by following patterns of behaviour that are stamped into our subconscious? How many of us follow modes of thinking we have inherited, which restrain our personal growth and do not allow our individual natures to flower? Look closely at two flowers of the same type, to the casual glance they look the same, however, upon closer inspection we will see that no two flowers are exactly alike. We as human beings are the same as a species but we all have a unique individual nature. Will you restrict your personal growth living by the examples that are imprinted in your subconscious? Or will you raise yourself up and be the best you can be. Our brains are like computers, in the sense that what we put in is what we get out. If your programming is holding you back, why not change it? Reality, your reality, could be whatever you want it to be. You don't have to accept anyone else's perception of what you should be. The supreme spirit/God gave us as human beings the power of reason. By using that power to look at ourselves, if we do not like what we see; we can change it and create our own reality. Henry Ford who brought the motor car into the price range of the general public once said: 'If you think you can't or if you think you can you're probably right'.

This life is precious, live it, step outside and embrace the unknown. A ship is safe and secure in harbour, but that is not what ships were made for. They are made for traveling the seas, where they sometimes encounter bad weather. They are built to surmount this restriction and travel on to the their destination. A ship safe in a harbour, never moving into the sea serves no purpose and never will, until it is put to sea and made use of.

Risk the high seas and live a life of your choosing. Embrace the bad things that come your way, you have the strength to overcome. Don't let fear hold you back, sapping your energy. Stagnation improves you not one iota and eventually you become bitter for not having made the effort to change.

Everything in nature is in constant change, balancing on a fine line. Face adversity and work through it to your true destination. Finding your unique talent, once you know that, you can add to the sum of human advancement and fulfill the reason for your existence. I believe we are all unique and in possession of talents. Talents that we are supposed to use to further our own development whilst adding to the pot of human progression.

Move away from the shore, follow your dreams, meet the challenges and enjoy the rewards for your courage.

Staying safe improves the quality of your life experience not one iota. Be brave, move away from the shore and enjoy the journey into uncharted waters.

~~~

To Flow Or Not To Flow?

THAT IS THE QUESTION, OR IS IT THE ANSWER?

Taoism, expressed as following the way, or going with the flow, is often misunderstood. I once read that the difference between Buddhism and Taoism was that, if a Buddhist were walking down a path through a valley and came to a river with no bridge or other means of crossing, he would jump in with the object of reaching the other side. The Taoist, however, would jump in and flow with the river to see where it took him.

At the time I agreed with this description wholeheartedly. Being primarily interested in Taoism and this being the source of most of my reading and practical studies at the time, this hypothesis suited my thoughts. For I believed at that time, that to follow the Taoist path meant to submit yourself to the way. To flow unresistingly with the path of one's own destiny. Therefore this little story appealed to my own beliefs, and was founded on my arrogant view that Taoism was superior to Buddhism. Indeed a true hypothesis, because it was based on opinion not fact. But what did I care, it confirmed my beliefs so it must be right, mustn't it? I told the story to other practitioners of Tai Chi and related Taoist arts, and those who were interested in the story confirmed that the reasoning was sound. Others were not interested, or perhaps not in agreement. But under the deluge of my enthusiasm for the validity of the story, put up no resistance. After all, I was a senior instructor under a Taoist master. I must be right, mustn't I? All this confirmed my belief, enforced that what I had always known to be true, was in fact correct.

During a weekend course I told the story to a group in the tea break, with extra enthusiasm for the story because my master was seated in the group. I glanced furtively in his direction now and then to judge his reaction. At first I met with a blank stare, and as I told my story I embellished it with loyalty to the cause. I was a Taoist through and through and would defend the cause relentlessly. As I finished I looked at my master and he smiled at me. I recognized that smile. I had seen it many times before and I knew what it meant. It meant I WAS RIGHT. Many years passed before I learnt the truth. That smile did not mean what I thought it meant at all. That smile meant, I can see you have made your mind up that you're right, and nobody is going to convince you otherwise. One day you will learn to listen more. For how can you learn by talking, telling others what you know does not increase YOUR knowledge. To learn more yourself, you must watch and listen, to people, to nature, to life. Only in this way, can you increase your store of understanding and wisdom. As time went by I noticed my master listened more than he talked, speaking quietly every now and then, when he felt he had something of value to add to the conversation, and of course in answer to the questions of those who were wise enough to ask them.

Those who talk incessantly at people, rather than converse with them, decrease their store of knowledge without putting much back in. If you take something out without putting anything back in, you will soon have an empty vessel. I think we have all met someone like this, at some time in our lives. An 'I know it all', who waffles constantly about what they are doing and what they know, without ever listening to the other person. Well I was like that a little then, and still am sometimes, when I forget myself. However, I know enough now to know that: 'Happiness is an inside job', and I am very, very happy. I find life exciting and wonderful. The more I learn, the more there seems to be to learn. I no longer become maniacally obsessed with my goals, the journey, the here and now is the exciting bit, that is where life is, in the present. By that, I certainly do not mean you should not have goals and dreams of a better future, for if you do not have anything to strive for you lose that zest for life. Life without struggle is life without vitality.

Everything in nature struggles to survive. Yet there are those who believe in a completely socialistic state, where people are cared for by the state, from the cradle to the grave. They are in my opinion, stifling the wonderful possibilities of creative living that all people are capable of. Taking the responsibility to look after people, in the belief that they cannot so for themselves is arrogant and egotistical. However, there are of course some sections of society that we should all endeavour to assist. For instance, the elderly and infirm being no longer able to care for themselves, and in this way we can show our compassion. But we must not mollycoddle all who are afraid and lack confidence. Instead, I believe we should teach and praise those who are willing to try to be responsible for their own financial, spiritual and physical well-being. Encourage people to take more personal responsibility. Not through harsh laws and regulations, but through a genuine love to see our fellow man/woman reach his/her full potential.

Nelson Mandela said in his Inaugural speech in 1994:

OUR DEEPEST FEAR

IS NOT THAT WE ARE INADEQUATE.

OUR DEEPEST FEAR

IS THAT WE ARE POWERFUL BEYOND MEASURE.

IT IS OUR LIGHT, NOT OUR DARKNESS THAT MOST

FRIGHTENS US.

WE ASK OURSELVES, 'WHO AM I TO BE TALENTED AND FABULOUS?' ACTUALLY, WHO ARE YOU NOT TO BE?

YOU ARE A CHILD OF GOD.

YOUR PLAYING SMALL DOES NOT SERVE THE WORLD.

THERE IS NOTHING ENLIGHTENED ABOUT SHRINKING SO THAT OTHER PEOPLE WONT FEEL INSECURE AROUND YOU.

WE WERE BORN TO MANIFEST THE GLORY OF GOD THAT IS WITHIN US: IT IS NOT JUST IN SOME OF US, IT IS IN EVERYONE.

AND AS WE LET OUR OWN LIGHT SHINE, WE UNCONSCIOUSLY GIVE OTHER PEOPLE PERMISSION TO DO THE SAME.

AS WE ARE LIBERATED FROM OUR FEARS, OUR PRESENCE AUTOMATICALLY LIBERATES OTHERS.

Surely we should encourage and assist others to flower and let out their individual splendor for all to see and enjoy. Will this not create the belief that perhaps, just perhaps, we can all achieve some of those dreams we harbour in our innermost thoughts. Should we not be able to share these things with our friends? Shouldn't we be encouraging each other to shine forth, savoring and relishing each other's achievements and triumphs as if they were our own? I think we should. There is far too much criticism, too much division, too much suppression of talent through negative thoughts.

Let's go back to our Taoist, following the flow of the river.

Does he merely float along completely unresistingly? I think not. For did not The Tao/God give our Taoist the gift of reason. Should he ignore this gift, and when the river threatens to throw his body against a rock allow that to happen? Knowing full well, that his flesh and blood body is too soft to sustain no damage from the collision, yet not soft enough to fragment and flow round it on contact, like the water can. Or should he use his power of reason and endeavour to steer himself clear of the obstruction, so he can continue his journey in good health? And if, like in life, he finds himself caught in the current and drawn into an eddy, should he stop there waiting for a storm to cause the river to flood and set him free? Or should he exert himself and battle his way out of the whirlpool that restricts his progress along his chosen path?

Only dead fish go with the flow of the river. Are you a dead fish, allowing decaying orthodox convention to rule your life, or are you alive and dancing to your own tune?

When the clouds burst and water falls to earth as rain, it begins its journey back to the sea. When we burst forth from our mothers womb, we begin our journey back to the supreme spirit/God. The rain soaks into the ground and emerges again forming mountain streams that dance down the hillside towards the sea. Along the way growing in size and depth. We as finite physical beings grow both physically and in knowledge. Although our physical abilities reach a peak and then decline, the knowledge and wisdom we acquire during our journey back to the supreme spirit, cannot be taken away. Like the stream, young children learn to maneuver round objects, laughing and dancing along with life. Sometimes resisting the natural path, they oppose obstructions and get hurt by taking this course of action. This is the natural learning process of life.

As the stream becomes a river, deeper, more complete, its choices of the path it takes expand, because of its greater volume and depth. As humans, as we grow expanding our knowledge and wisdom, we create for ourselves a discernment and profoundness, which multiplies our choices in life.

Ultimately the river returns to the sea, the seawater evaporates, along with moisture from the earth, to form clouds and returns to the earth again as rain. This process represents the transitory. So we live our lives and then we die, we cease to exist and fade away. Like the clouds cease to exist and become rain, and the rain becomes the rivers and then returns to the sea. I believe that we live our lives then cease to exist, fade away. Merely changing form, leaving behind the heavy, dull, physical body, our spirit returns to the infinite existence. Until it is time for us to be born again, to this finite earth. I believe we must live many lives to refine and purify our spirits, before we return to our ultimate source, the supreme spirit/God. Each round of existence we are granted is precious, not to be wasted. Life is a gift from the supreme spirit/God the Almighty. How we live it, is our gift to God.

So this precious gift should not be squandered while we aimlessly drift through life. I believe we should endeavour to learn as much as we can about ourselves. Developing ourselves to our maximum potential, so that we can be more useful to society. For if we all developed ourselves a little more, would not humanity as a whole be greatly benefited? Taoism is about doing things and what better ethos for humanity than the service of others.

Thomas Edison said: If we did all we are capable of doing we would literally astonish ourselves.

While Thomas Edison was striving to invent the light bulb,

someone once asked him why he continued when he had already failed 1000 times. He replied I haven't failed, I just found 1000 ways it will not work. You cannot stop a spirit imbued with that kind of tenacity. And because he continued until he was successful, we have the benefit of the electric light bulb, and what service to humanity he provided in the process. Just imagine, without Thomas Edison's relentless pursuance of his goal, we would still be lighting our way through the darkness with a candle. Thomas Edison's destiny was to be an inventor, but he didn't just flow with his destiny, he worked hard at it, he struggled with it, and he worked at his inventions. He dreamed of a better tomorrow in which he played a part, through his talents as an inventor.

Thomas Edison also declared, 'I never did a day's work in my life. It was all fun.' Now there is an attitude we could all do to emulate.

So should we flow or not flow, with the stream of life? I believe we should flow with life, in the sense that we need to learn to recognize our unique God given talents and then use them as best we can. This I believe will allow us to expand our own self-development, and in the process we will be able to serve our fellow man to the best of our abilities. However, when life puts obstacles in our way, I believe we should circumvent them. When life presents us with problems, I believe we should find solutions. We each and every one of us, unique manifestations of the supreme spirit. Let us live our lives with courage and passion. We can accomplish all we can imagine, for if it were not possible we would not be able to imagine it. God gave us this ability and presumably he expects us to use it.

With the right intention, i.e. to improve the circumstances of our peers, let us strive to accomplish all we can conceive in our minds. Let us leave nothing undone. When we depart this earth let us be all used up, let us leave nothing in reserve. It is such a shame to hear people say 'I wish I had done so and so when I had the chance.' Let us embrace opportunity and live our lives to the full, for none of us shall walk this path again. Even if we did, it would not be the same, for as the Greek philosopher Heraclitus observed, 'You cannot step twice into the same river, for other water is continually flowing in.'

Live life to the full in the present, nurture grand expectations of your future. Keep nothing in reserve, give of yourself unstintingly, and your life will be a glorious existence, and just payment, for the gift of life bestowed upon you by the divine creator.

~~~

You Cannot Fail All The Time

How we view ourselves, is one of the most important ingredients in the kind of life we live. Think about it, if you do not love yourself - you will not love others. If you are not kind to yourself - you will not be kind to others. Sure you can pretend to love others, and pretend to be kind. But Taoism is about reality, the way things are, and if you deceive yourself you guarantee yourself unhappiness. Still, you could pretend that you are happy, and many people do; but they fool only themselves. Well that's easy to understand and I see what you're getting at, you may say, and I can see the commonsense of your response. But you don't understand what a hard time I have had in the past. My childhood was difficult, I had lousy parents, I was bullied, I was an only child and pitifully shy. And now I'm stuck in a job I hate, I don't get on with my partner, I still have problems with my parents, etc.

Well my friend, the only thing you can truly take control of, is yourself. It is the development of yourself and the control of your ego, that will change the world into the beautiful, exciting place it is. You are a child of the universe, there is nothing greater than yourself, you can become, all you want to be. Do you realize you are unique, out of the millions and millions of people who inhabit this planet; there is not one other exactly like you. The Tao made you that special.

If you look at nature you will see that nature never complains, it accepts all conditions, and with patience and persistence continues to endure and flourish. Animals and plant life do not complain when they get lashed by the cold rain, for they know the rain is necessary to their existence. The fish do not complain when storms and pollution disrupt their environment.

So you've had a rough time in the past, or things are against you now. What can you do about it? Well you could blame others, pointing the finger at their faults and failures, demanding a change in their behaviour. Wave your arms about and shout at them. However, it says in section 38 the first chapter of De, or Life in The Tao Te Ching: Whosoever cherishes morality acts and if someone does not respond to him he waves his arms about and pulls him up. It goes on to say morality is the penury of faith and trust and the beginning of confusion. So this criticism and blame of others is separation from the Tao.

To follow the Tao, we must endeavour to purify our thoughts and help others, with acts of kindness and love. This is only possible if you are able to love yourself, because you cannot give to others what you yourself do not possess. So we must start with ourselves, our own spirit. My teacher used to say that you should cultivate yourself physically, mentally and spiritually, and that you must start with the spirit. Now to make these changes is not easy. It will require persistent and dedicated action on your part, to replace the bad thought habits built up through many years of conditioning. You see most of us are told many times, by well-meaning parents and friends throughout our lives, 'You couldn't do that' or 'You best not try that, you'll only be disappointed if it doesn't work out'.

Freedom of action, fueled by a confident belief in your God given abilities, is what is required to move you out of a drab existence and into the real world. The truly authentic existence, where opportunity and happiness are available in abundance. So start to improve yourself by studying. How? Read biographies of successful happy people, don't say I can't be bothered to read stuff like that. Remember, a man who can read but doesn't is no better than one who can't.

Look at the people you meet at work or in your leisure time, see the happy one's and study them. Read the Tao Te Ching and other books on philosophy or self-improvement, until you find those you enjoy and relate to. The most important thing to understand is to do it NOW. The beginning of a happier life FOR YOU, starts RIGHT NOW. The power to change your life for the better lies with you, because God gave you the power of reason, but you must use it. Use it wisely, decide that today is the first day of the rest of your life, and that it is going to be exciting, rewarding and fun. Don't say 'I'm too stuck in my ways'. Life is movement, growth, expansion. Do not be one of the living dead. Cast off that caterpillars cocoon that restricts your choices and movement in life, become the butterfly and soar to wherever and whatever you want. The kind of life you lead is within your own control, but you must pick up the reins and drive your chariot to your own personal victory. Make the decision to do it now. As I said in the previous chapter, life is a gift from God - How you live it, is your gift to God. The past is gone, let it go, the future awaits you. WHAT WILL YOU BECOME?

An old Chinese proverb says: The best time to plant a tree is twenty years ago, the second best time is NOW.

Don't listen to the skeptics who tell you to keep your nose clean and your head down. In my opinion the meaning and value of life is simple this:- Living life without fear and putting your trust in the Supreme spirit/God.

These words were printed on the back of a church bulletin by an anonymous writer, but they are full of wisdom for those who fear failure:

Lord, are you trying to tell me something?

For failure does not mean I'm a failure;

It does mean I have not yet succeeded.

Failure does not mean I have accomplished nothing;

It does mean that I have learnt something.

Failure does not mean I've been disgraced;

It does mean I dared to try.

Failure does not mean I don't have it;

It does mean I have to do something in a different way.

Failure does not mean that I have wasted my life;

It does mean that I have a reason to start over.

Failure does not mean that I should give up;

It does mean I should try harder.

Failure does not mean that I will never make it;

It does mean that I need more patience.

Failure does not mean you have abandoned me;

It does mean you must have another idea.

The title of this chapter is 'You cannot fail all the time'. But as far as Taoism is concerned, this statement is nonsense. Because failure and success are opposites, and as such, are separate from the Tao, the one principle. Yet they are a part of this existence here on Earth, because on Earth we live in a state of duality, and through our experience of this duality we can render ourselves glimpses of the true Tao, the supreme spirit, the one principle.

So this discussion of opposites is necessary to glean understanding. Do not be discouraged if it all seems too much and you feel perplexed. For it is through this confusion that wisdom emerges. For does not the light of day, spring forth from the darkness of the night? Does not the warmth and vigor of summer, follow the cold and bleakness of winter? The greater the wisdom you attain, the greater will be your contribution to life, and the greater will be your love of the Supreme spirit/God.

Chapter seven of the Tao Te Ching states:

Heaven is eternal and Earth lasting.

They are lasting and eternal because they do not live for themselves.

Therefore can they live forever. Thus also is the Man of Calling:

He disregards himself, and his Self is increased.

He gives himself away and his Self is preserved.

Is it not true: because he desires nothing as his own, he is complete?

This seems at first thought to repudiate the self-development and enhancement of the material world, through the development of new technologies/medicines etc. However, I do not believe so. I believe the message is quite different. I believe we should endeavour to improve living conditions for all the people of the world, but not at the expense of nature. We must work with nature, by all means harvesting her bounteous gifts, but without greed. For as the Tao Te Ching says: Heaven is eternal and Earth lasting. And if we rape and pillage the Earth's resources through greed, we will deny ourselves the life sustaining necessities of clean air, water and food, and kill ourselves off. But the Earth will endure and eventually cleanse itself. However, if we instead choose to follow the example of nature. And give of ourselves, as it says in chapter seven of the Tao Te Ching: He gives himself away and his Self is preserved. Then we will harvest nature's bounty, without destroying its ability to replenish itself. For we exist side by side, interdependent on each other, if nature flourishes so do we and the animal kingdom. If we restrict natures process, reducing its ability to replenish itself well, we reduce the quality of our own life. This is the way, everything affects everything else. Nature gives unstintingly: nothing in nature exists for itself in isolation. Therefore it can live for eternity.

So it would seem working for the good of others could be one interpretation of the message of this chapter. And a lack of material possessions is indicated by the following don't you think?

I myself subscribed to that view for a good few years. However, I would like to share my present understanding with you. Firstly desiring nothing, is not the same as having nothing. And if you wish to help others by providing things they do not have, then as far as providing, support, care and love are concerned, you yourself must possess them. As for the material things that you would provide for their needs, if you do not possess them, from where will they come? Should we create a fuss and demand the government, the rich, a country better off than ours provide them. Is this not morality?

Section 38 of the Tao Te Ching says of morality: morality is the penury of faith and trust.

So demanding others do the providing, does not seem to be in accordance with the Tao. Many who complain that others are not providing this or that for the less fortunate, whilst doing nothing themselves, surely must be hypocritical. If they really cared, would they not work to provide the necessities and then give them to the needy. A very wealthy man I once heard speak, told this story of his sister. She said to him one day. 'Money doesn't make you happy.' to which he replied.

'You're right, money doesn't guarantee happiness, but it can alleviate a lot of misery.'

She then said, 'If I had your wealth I would give it all away.'

To which he replied, 'That's not true, because if you loved people that much, you would be doing something to help them now, and you are not.'

I would like to add that this man has for a long time, and to this day, continues to support many charities and good causes. The cynical would say well it's easy for him, he's got plenty of money. Well that was not always so, he worked hard doing what others were not prepared to do, and reaped the rewards because of those efforts, that others were not entitled to have, and now chooses to help others. He helps those who are unable to help themselves i.e. the sick and infirm, and he helps those who want to help themselves, but lack the resources to achieve their aims. Helping them to take responsibility for their own futures, as he says he was helped by many along the way.

You see I believe there is nothing wrong with money, money is, after all, only a means of barter, that is not subject to decay (disregarding inflation of course). Those who develop a greed for amassing wealth for wealth's sake, I believe, ensure the degeneration of their own spirit and a loss of the nectar of life. But creating wealth, and then using that wealth for a right principle, such as the freeing of people from the scourge of poverty by providing employment. Or the attainment of a lofty goal, such as the providing of medical supplies and the funds to build hospitals etc. These cannot be people who are heartless scrooges, as often depicted in the newspapers, or on TV.

Surely, it must be the intention that is the essence of our spirituality, and therefore our love towards our fellow man. Money, or the lack of it, doesn't make you virtuous. It is the content of your heart, not your bank balance, that shows who you are. Rich or poor, you cannot hide that, for it is there for all to see, in your actions. Words mean little, it is the doing that counts. I am reminded of a quote I heard recently:

> Give a man a fish and feed him for a day.

> Teach a man to fish and feed him for life!

If you really want to help people, you must teach them to become self-reliant, obvious exceptions being the old, sick and infirm. Although, many in this category have achieved for themselves amazing success, the eminent scientist Stephen William Hawkins for one. The understanding I received from my Master, of the best way to help others, was to teach by example. This is the natural way in the wild, parents teach their young to hunt, fish, and the other skills required for survival. We must do the same and release the unlimited capacity of the human spirit to excel. Replace fear and constriction, by encouragement and freedom and who knows what we, the human race as a whole, are capable of. It is said that we only use a tenth of our conscious minds. What would we achieve if we coaxed another ten or twenty percent out? Then, by working together in harmony, what could we achieve? The possibilities are beyond comprehension, and so would be the benefits to mankind.

The world needs achievers to solve the problems of the world. People, who through a genuine love of mankind, can make great progress. For there must be movement, without it there would be stagnation, and stagnation leads to death. Stop the flow of your blood and you start moving away from life. We need people who can help the development of mankind whilst keeping the tenuous balance of nature secure. Encouragement for everyone to increase their God given abilities to the full, would this not increase the lot of mankind in general?

Theodore Roosevelt described the kind of people who deserve to be recognized as achievers when he wrote:

It's not the critic who counts; not the man who points out how the strong man stumbled, or where the doer of deeds could have done better.

The credit belongs to the man who is actually in the arena, whose face is marred by dust and sweat and blood; who strives valiantly; who errs and comes short again and again, who knows the great enthusiasms, the great devotions and spends himself in a worthy cause; who at best knows the triumphs of high achievement; and who, at worst, if he fails, at least fails while daring greatly, so that his place shall never be with those cold and timid souls who know neither victory nor defeat.

So whatever your dreams are, dare to dream them, and then ignore the critics and go for it. If you are determined and focused, you will succeed. For as the chapters heading says 'You cannot fail all the time'. So if you don't give up, you will succeed, and the world needs your spirited example. You, by daring to live a life full of vivacious action in pursuit of your goals, will give permission to others to dare to follow your example. Life is action, not standing back and watching others, perhaps criticizing, any fool can criticize. No, like the Taoist, why not jump in the river and see where it takes you. But steer yourself clear of any obstacles that may cause you harm, when you can. You will undoubtedly get a bump or two on your journey, but oh! the wonderful things you will do and the magnificent things you will see. Life is for living, it is the journey that is the prize, not the destination, destination is death. The journey is life, enjoy it, contribute and make your maker proud.

Don't forget the goal, for without a purpose to give you focus, you will wander aimlessly achieving little. Remember, even the Taoists of old had a goal, enlightenment. Whatever your goal, no one can stop you achieving it, but you. If you stop, you fail, if you continue relentlessly until you get it, you succeed. It's as simple as that. Whatever you desire, you can have. As it says in Ecclesiastics 1:4: A generation comes, a generation goes, but The Earth abides.

Go for it, achieve for yourself and your family, the qualities and lifestyle you want. What kind of qualities or lifestyle you want, is a personal decision. God gave you the power to make your own decisions, use it. Have the courage to take control of your life and become an example to others, of the infinite possibilities available to us all. I believe anything you can dream of, is attainable. As a child, I remember people used to joke saying 'Oh yeah and one day a man will go to the moon'. Well it's not a joke anymore, because someone dared to dream it was possible and set about putting that dream into reality. Whatever the mind can conceive, man can achieve. Whatever kind of life you want, you can have, because only you can stop you. You may not succeed the first, second, third, fourth, fifth or even sixth time you try, but if you persevere you will attain your heart's desire. Why? Because you cannot fail all the time, the law of averages will cut in sooner or later, and success will be yours. If you could look through a photograph album of you and your life, five or ten years from now, what would you like to see? That's your dream, now you know where you want to go, make it a certainty by taking action now. An old Chinese proverb comes to mind: A thousand mile journey starts with the first step.

Take those steps one at a time and even a thousand mile journey is possible. If you could add up all the miles you have walked so far in your life, what would the total be? Well as an example, if you walked on average only 5 miles a day, (and I assure you, that isn't a lot when you add up all the little trips, up and down stairs, to the shops and back, at work etc.) 5 miles a day x 7 days a week x 52 weeks a year x 25 years is a staggering 45,500 miles. Quite a lot eh! A few steps at a time, not very noticeable, but when added together over time, amount to an epic journey. What sights, what knowledge, what achievements could you gain from such a voyage.

Any success you have achieved so far in your life, is made up of little actions, strung together. Your future success is the same, big successes are not usually giant steps, but little ones and lots of them. Set your goals, know where you want to go, and take one step at a time, in that direction. Don't try to run too fast, in the hope that you will get there instantly, you will simply wear yourself out. Remember to have a rest now and then, remember the story of the tortoise and the hare. Don't dawdle either, study the river, sometimes it rushes over rocks and through narrow gorges, and at other times it flows unimpeded along its path. But the river is always moving forwards, sometimes moving this way and that to avoid obstructions, occasionally its path is blocked and it has to gather strength and volume until it can flow over the obstacle and continue its journey. But always moving on, for that is the essence of life, continual movement. Anything that comes to a standstill, starts to stagnate and decay. Too many people give up control of their lives to others and get directed about, for the whole of their time here on earth, by their relations, their boss etc. They follow each other like sheep. We are not sheep. We are a unique species with enormous potential.

Don't just dream your dreams, like most people do, live them. Take one small step at a time and you will get there. When the supreme spirit sees you are dedicated and sincere in your quest, you will get all the assistance you need. Have patience remember that if you try to grow too fast, you will lack the inner strength to endure the trials awaiting you, along your journey. For when you reach your destination, you will see another greater vision of your future, and in your growth and achievement, you will inspire and uplift others to achieve and grow also. Be the best you can be, that is all the supreme spirit requires of you. Let your gift to the supreme spirit/God be, to live the most magnificent life you can.

~~~

Me And My Shadow

The sun casts a shadow over things, or rather the things by their existence produce their own shadow. The supreme spirit/God generates only light. We are a manifestation of that light. We come from the light and we will return to the light. We carry a shadow within us, our ego, and when we turn away from the light, our shadow is fabricated. Its existence dulls the beauty around us, and clouds our minds to the purity of thought. Dark thoughts start to take hold in the mind, as the pure light is blocked.

When we walk with the light behind us on a sunny day, we cast a shadow, this shadow is a replica of our body, it mirrors our image, but it is not the real self. Our shadow can become larger or smaller than our actual physical size, depending on the angle of the light in relation to our body. As we walk away from the light, we can clearly see our shadow spread before us. As children, most of us found our shadows fascinating, spending many hours experimenting in play with it. Perhaps it is this fascination with this other identity, which leads us to create a persona that we feel will be acceptable to others. As teenagers, not knowing our true self, many of us create a personality based on a famous person who we admire. Many of our children copy hairstyles, dress-like and imitate the behaviour of TV characters or pop idols. Wishing to identify themselves, with the exciting lifestyles these people appear to have. And then later as adults, we mimic people we admire or people we wish to identify with. People in positions of power, people with attributes or qualities, we would like for ourselves. Why do we seek outward appraisal and approval? At an early age, most of us gain approval for imitating others, and hear references like 'He looks just like his uncle with that haircut' or

'She looks just like cousin Mary in that dress' etc. We seek approval and respect, through following codes of behaviour or dress to conform to the status quo, though not necessarily that of our parents.

Many Taoist principles are represented by the study of water. The colour of water is altered as a result of sediment, or dissolved animal and plant pigment, or both. We as human beings are approximately 98% water, astrologically water governs the emotions. How we feel emotionally about something, affects the way we think. The way we think, affects the way we act, the way we act gives others their opinion or insight into us as a person. The condition of the sky also alters the colour of the water, just as others opinions of us (if we allow them), effects our perception of ourselves. We all receive many remarks and advice from people, friends, relations, loved ones and people we work with. Sadly much of it is negative, given in good faith by well-meaning people, who believe they are helping us.

However, negative feedback reduces our self-confidence. I believe we should consider this freely given advice, but not hang on to it, allowing it to erode our self confidence. But let it pass by, like clouds on a dull day, blown by the breeze. Just as calm water allows the sediment in it, to sink. By bringing our minds under our control, not allowing ourselves to be adversely affected by the conclusions of others. In this way our opinion of ourselves and our path/way remains clear and unimpeded, by the sediment of others convictions.

Another attribute that affects the colour of water, is its depth. The deeper the water, the less it is affected by sediment and discolouration. Close to the shore the sea picks up much sediment, sand, discarded rubbish and pollution. The surface of a river witnesses the most disruption. We, if we nurture the inner, create a depth that cannot be polluted by the sediment of others opinions and actions, we remain entire. In this state we are in communion with the Tao. If our actions come from within, they will always be appropriate.

As it says in the Tao TE Ching:

One looks for it and does not see it:

Its name is 'seed'.

One listens for it and does not hear it:

Its name is 'subtle'.

One reaches for it and does not feel it:

Its name is 'small'.

These three cannot be separated,

Therefore, intermingled they form the one.

Its highest is not light,

Its lowest is not dark.

Welling up without interruption,

One cannot name it.

It returns again to non-existence.

This is called the formless form,

The objectless image.

This is called the darkly chaotic.

Walking towards it, one does not see its face;

following it, one does not see its back.

If one holds fast to the DAO of antiquity

In order to master today's existence

One may know the ancient beginning.

This means: Dao's continuous thread.

It is well worth reading this passage two or three times, and spending a little time in meditation over its meaning, before moving on.

So, empty and moved from within, our actions become the actions of the Tao/God. This is the state of mind of the child, a pure reaction to the conditions around it. Imbued with an internal curiosity, the child moves on, eager to experience life, marveling at the wonder of the world. This is the state the Taoist seeks, the childlike nature, tempered with the wisdom of the ages. Ever watchful for that shadow, our ego, lest we turn away from the light in forgetfulness and once again fabricate its being. Ever mindful, in a permanent state of meditation, ever receptive to the supreme spirit's universal energy. This I wish for myself, so that I may help others attain it. My master showed the way forward, now it is up to me to follow the path.

When you know what you have been, then look deep inside yourself to learn who you are now, then and only then, can you consider what you want to be in the future. You can say as many people do 'I am who I am' and then this becomes reality for you. But, are you who you think you are? When we walk into the shadow of a building, our own shadow disappears, or is it merely hidden from view. When we associate with people who turn away from the supreme spirit, our own essence becomes dull and dark. When we enter the shadows in this way, we lose sight of the eternal light. Surrounded by lost souls, we become lost ourselves. The essence of our true self being blunted, we lose the true nectar of life.

In one of the episodes of the 'Kung Fu' TV series (first aired in the 1970's) Kwai Chang Caine asks the Abbot of the Shaolin monastery, why one of the masters took his own life. The Abbott leads Kwai Chang Caine to a parapet on the monastery wall, and pointing to the surrounding countryside said to the boy, 'Tell me what you see.'

Kwai Chang said, 'Great beauty, Master.'

The Abbot said, 'Our unfortunate Master, saw only ugliness.'

'How is that possible?' said Kwai Chang.

The Abbot simply replied. 'I do not know, like you, I see only the beauty and wonder of nature.'

What we see and experience, greatly influences us and everything has an effect on the way we feel, think and therefore, act. If we surround ourselves with dull and negative people, spend our time complaining of what is wrong with our lives and placing the blame at others feet. Then we will experience much unhappiness and sorrow in our lives. However, if we can see the beauty in nature, and appreciate our own unique individuality, expressing this in our own lives in an unashamed and generous way. Does this not give praise to the supreme spirit and rejoicing in the gift of life?

When you cast no shadow, but reflect the pure light from within, separated no longer, reunited with your spirit, then you will have found your personal Tao. Life will become happy and harmonious, and you will be a living example to others. Your actions will always be appropriate, you will be able to help many people in little ways, that will affect their lives deeply. This is the Tao, action in non-action.

As more and more people return to spiritual values, the dark shadows that have fallen on the earth will disperse, and peace and harmony will radiate across the globe. But, as my master used to say 'to reach the spirit, you must start with yourself'. We cannot always control externally what is happening, but we can control internally i.e. ourselves. Instead of pointing out the many injustices in the world, if we all increased our spiritual values a little, the accumulative effect would be to exalt the human population beyond measure. This all requires much effort individually for us all, but is it worth it? I believe it is. I know from personal experience, that as I have striven to improve myself, the benefits to my personal happiness have been outstanding. Searching not outward but looking within, mostly it is a painful process, especially at the start. But like most things, if you persevere it gets easier, and I assure you the rewards are worth the effort.

~~~

Tao The Essence

To seek inner calm - to find The Tao - to meditate - to reach universal consciousness, is the goal of many seekers of the truth. These are available to all who's intentions are pure; and yet at the same time it is impossible, because there is always more - always a deeper understanding to be gleaned, always a little more to be learnt. To imagine that you have ever reached complete knowledge, is egotism and death. A zombie does not experience life in any meaningful way, neither is it any longer, a sentient being. To live is to perceive, to feel, to experience, to learn, to develop and therefore progress. So seekers of the truth must do just that, seek, consistently and constantly, for there is no limit to the Tao. The seeker who believes he has found it all and indulges in cessation, dies and becomes a zombie. As it says in the 'Tao Te Ching' section 38:

Whosoever cherishes life, does not know about life. Therefore he has life.

Whosoever does not cherish life, seeks not to lose life; therefore he has no life.

For those not familiar with the 'Tao Te Ching', the second sentence refers to those who live only to please the senses. Amassing material possessions, seeking to raise themselves above others. Unable or unwilling to see the true nectar of life, these people experience conflict and unhappiness consistently. Whilst the first sentence points out, that those who seek not to greedily gather goods and pleasures, who instead seek to contribute to humanity in some way, these people experience happiness and learn to understand the true essence of life. There is much, much more meaning within these words and I fervently study the Tao Te Ching, so that I may learn more, understand more, so that I, too, may progress.

If one looks at the external things, one finds that the same principles that apply to the internal apply to the external. In mathematics, the science of numbers, to reach zero from any given number we must go backwards to the start, the essence. In the beginning, when we first learn about numbers, counting backwards to zero is easy. Later as we progress in our learning of numbers, we are introduced to decimals, and now we have extended the range between 1 and 0 now we can have .09-.08-.07 etc., until we reach .00. Which we could call ultimate zero, the finale root. Yet this is not so, for we can expand upon this by extending .00, we can have .009-.008-.007 etc., until we reach .000. And again we can repeat this process stating at .0009 and so on. We can do this, because mathematics has no limits, any that are there, are put there by mans limited mind. If you were so inclined, you could repeat the above process over and over infinitely, without ever arriving at a final solution to absolute zero.

If you wish to meditate to seek inner calm - to find The Tao - to reach universal consciousness or whatever name you attribute to the process of spiritual self development, this I believe is easy and available to all, whose intentions are pure. To learn who you really are and put yourself in touch with the essence, your true source. This process of internal development, is like the example given using mathematics. First you must learn to work backwards to one, yourself. Then, once you have put yourself in touch with your own body and mind, and learnt to bring these under your own conscious control, then and only then, can you progress beyond towards the essence, your true source. Like the decimal system of mathematics, there are many levels of accomplishment. When you reach a level, do not delude yourself that you have reached the final solution, but be grateful for what you have received so far, in the knowledge that there is always more.

Remember too, that balance in all things is essential, if we are to progress. We looked at the mathematics of the small, and saw that the smallest number could be made smaller and smaller without end. And so if we look at its opposite, by making a number larger by adding to it $1+1=2$ - $2+1=3$ - $3+1=4$ etc., again we can do this indefinitely. So, I believe, we must expand ourselves externally as well as internally, and the balance between the two, must be our own choice. If we become so obsessed with the internal, the spiritual side of life, that we drift into a fantasy world. We will become prisoners within our own minds and ostracize ourselves from society and therefore be unable to contribute, in any meaningful way. If we become so obsessed with the external things of this world, that we lose our control and become slaves to our desire to please the senses. Freely feeding them on whatever we want, with no regard to the effect on others, or our own health. Again we exclude ourselves from society, and set an example that is unhelpful to global harmony, or the education of our children. We must I believe, take responsibility for ourselves, NOT expect someone else to do it for us.

If we all concerned ourselves with our own development internally and externally, resisting the temptation to direct others by force into our way of thinking. There would be less conflict within our own homes, towns, countries, world and there would be much more harmony around the globe. Of course all this is easy to understand, but very difficult to put into practise. And that is the crux of the matter, putting into practise what we learn, contributing, adding to the pot, is what development and progress is all about. If we refuse to take responsibility for ourselves, only taking and never giving, we will have nothing of any value. If however we contribute in whatever way we can, giving freely of ourselves, then the more we give the more we shall receive and the greater will be our value to humanity.

The tide comes in, the tide goes out. The tide operates not to a regular pattern, because the tide is influence by the movement of the moon and sun. The direct cause of the tide is the acceleration of the earth, as a response to the gravitational pull of the moon and sun. The moon and sun move in accordance with conditions prevalent within our solar system, they move as a response to their place and the influences that affect them. And these influences that shape the movement of the moon and sun are of course stimulated by other influences too. In fact, as in the science of quantum mechanics and the chaos theory, everything is affected by everything else.

So man cannot influence nature, he cannot change the tides, or the behavior or the moon and sun. These things of nature are governed by the Tao, the essence. Man can and does watch nature. In the past, within the chaos that is the movement of the Tao, some gifted and learned men and women have seen patterns that recur over and over. Never, quite exactly the same, but near enough to be recognizable, when encountered again. The observations of these men and women have enabled us to construct tables, that guide us when we need to know, for instance, the times of the tides. As our knowledge of the behavior of the moon and sun are increased, we can modify the tables and increase their accuracy. So we have an ongoing process of, continual and never ending development and progress. And this is the Tao, the way, constant movement, life. Without this constant movement, life would be impossible. Consider what would happen if moisture did not rise up from the sea to form clouds, which then fall on the earth as rain. All living things need water to sustain life, without this movement of water, life on our planet would cease.

So the essence of life I think, is to be aware of what is happening to you and around you right now, and then react to those influences. If you try to change things because you find them unacceptable, you enter into conflict with the Tao; the way of your own destiny. We cannot change the tides or the way the stars and planets move within our solar system, this is ordained by the Tao. But, we can work within this framework and still have as much freedom as we wish. Yet, as all those who have to work with nature to earn their livelihood know, if you oppose nature you condemn yourself to continual conflict and misery.

We must give, in order to receive, if we all took and never gave, soon there would be nothing left, if we all gave and never accepted anything; very soon we would have nothing left to give. My teacher always taught me, that the Yin comes before the Yang i.e. you must give in order to receive. If you have a cup and the cup is full, you cannot put anything in it, if it is half empty you can then put something in it, if it is completely empty it can be completely filled again. The more completely you give of yourself; the more you are able to receive. Nature gives unstintingly of itself, so that life may continue and as it says in the bible Ecclesiastes 1:4

A generation comes, a generation goes, yet the earth stands firm for ever.

I believe that we were meant to use what nature provides for us but if we chop down trees, we must also plant replacement trees, otherwise we will deplete stocks until there are none left. If we plant again when we take, we will always have enough.

Be grateful for what you have been given, share it with others, in the process you will receive many gifts of friendship and much love. Be a willing servant to others, and the Tao will see that all your needs are satisfied.

Free your mind of fear and shortage and enjoy the pleasure of giving, so that you may receive a life of freedom. My Master, Chee Soo, taught me that if you can follow your own personal Tao, you will never have to worry about the mundane things of life. As once the Tao sees you are seeking to follow you own personal Tao without resistance, it will nurture you as you have never known; providing all that you need to complete your path.

~~~

To Eat or Not to Eat Meat?

This is a risky area, as diet it such an emotive subject, but I would like to add my two penny's worth.

The question of which diet is healthier, one including meat or one excluding meat, commonly referred to as a vegetarian diet, has been argued over the years with the supporters of eating meat, by far outnumbering the vegetarians.

The word vegetarian is not derived from vegetable, as most people think, but from the Latin word vegus, which means "full of life". Some of the world's greatest thinkers eschewed meat, among them: Leonardo Da Vinci, Sir Isaac Newton, St. Francis of Assisi and Albert Einstein who said: "It is my view that the vegetarian manner of living, by its purely physical effect on the human temperament, would most beneficially influence the lot of mankind."

Pythagoras, who is generally given credit for its inception, praised vegetarianism for its hygienic nature and the kinship it fostered, between man and the animals. In the past, most Doctors, nutritionists and those responsibly for health education, have in the main, stated that a diet which contained no meat, could not be a healthy diet. Because this kind of diet, would be lacking in certain minerals and vitamins, especially the B group of vitamins. In recent years, the trend towards eating less meat has increased, because the technology that has so successfully increased meat production, is an unnatural method. The use of chemicals and the unnatural living conditions the animals are kept in, which in many cases are appalling, are designed to force growth. People are now becoming increasingly concerned, about their intake of chemicals and fat, via the food chain.

Some scientists believe that the chemicals fed to these animals, will lead to an accelerated aging, in humans. We are constantly told by our doctors, that we must reduce our fat intake, to lower cholesterol levels. No food, in the plant world contains cholesterol. Using modern technology, nutritionists have shown that the body can obtain all it requires to remain healthy, without eating meat.

Many people now consider it wrong to kill animals for food, when this is not necessary for survival. Perhaps they feel as Leonardo Da Vinci did, when he said, "I have from an early age forsworn the use of meat, and the time will come, when men will look upon the slaughter of animals as they now look upon the slaughter of men."

The International Development Research Centre in Ottawa, claims meat production, in western countries, is cheating the rest of the world of much needed food. In view of this, eating meat is a wanton waste of resources. The amount of food an animal eats, is out of all proportion to the amount of eating meat it produces. In fact, the modern battery chicken, which is the most efficient in converting its food to flesh, takes around 12 pounds of food to produce 1 pound of meat (not including the bones). Pigs eat 20 pounds and cows 30 pounds of food, to produce one pound of meat. Sheep usually graze on land that is unsuitable for crops, and they are fortunate enough to roam free, at least, until market day. Every pound of food that is grown for feeding to animals, to produce eating meat, is a pound of food less for a person. So whilst we indulge ourselves in eating meat, others must go hungry.

Still we can always send our old clothes and perhaps an old blanket or two via Oxfam, to ease our consciences, perhaps even give a little of our hard earned cash. But whilst we try to cure the symptoms, instead of the cause, hoping the problem will go away or somebody else will sort it out, more people starve to death. But we are not really interested in tackling the cause, because it would involve altering our eating habits, and we must have our meat, our selfish greed robs us of our affection and compassion for our fellow man.

Scientific research has shown that, children born to vegetarian mothers are as healthy, as babies born to omnivore mothers. Still birth, premature deliveries and birth defects, occur no more or less frequently, in vegetarian women, than in any other particular group.

The strongest animals who possess the greatest endurance, the horse, the ox, the elephant, are all vegetarians, as are many of our world class sports people. The physical apparatus of humans is not like that, of a natural carnivore. They have sharp teeth and claws, for tearing flesh. Our teeth resemble more closely the vegetarian animals, which have flat molars for grinding. Furthermore, carnivores have short intestines, usually no more then three times the length of the trunk, so that meat can be quickly eliminated from the body, before it has had time to putrefy. Human intestines are huge, up to 12 times the length of the body, giving the meat plenty of time to turn rank inside the intestinal tract, and poison the consumer.

Social conditioning plays an enormous part in our eating habits, for instance, the thought of eating steak and kidney pie for breakfast may seem ridiculous, yet three hours later it is welcomed. Food snobbery is in evidence when foods like caviar and pheasant are valued, not because they are more nutritious foods, but because they cost more or are associated with the upper classes. Food advertiser's play on our emotions, by conjuring up pleasant memories or confirming social images associated with the consumption of their products, all in an effort to sell more. We must resist these temptations, for the good of our health.

The Irish playwright George Bernard Shaw, himself a vegetarian, was once very ill. His doctors warned him, that unless he began to eat eggs and drink a broth made with a meat base, he would die. Rather than heed the doctors advice, Shaw called for his private secretary. In the doctors presence Shaw dictated his final instructions: 'I solemnly declare that it is my last wish, that when I am no longer a captive of this physical body, that my coffin when carried to the graveyard be accompanied by mourners of the following categories: first birds; second, sheep, lambs, cows, and other animals of the kind; third, live fish in an aquarium. Each of these mourners should carry a placard bearing the inscription: 'O lord, be gracious to our benefactor George Bernard Shaw, who gave his life for saving ours!' George Bernard Shaw also once said, "Mankind will never have peace until we stop killing and eating animals."

I think he is probably right too. For if we cannot show animals love and respect, allowing them to live out their lives naturally. I do not see how we can ever truly learn, to love and respect each other. If this is so, then we shall never end the continual conflict and misery that we impose upon one another, in our continual struggle for personal prosperity. If we are to live together in peace and co-operation, we must first stop eating meat.

Many foods that have beneficial qualities, also contain properties that are not good for the human body. Meat which contains many minerals and proteins, also introduces large amounts of cholesterol, high concentrations of which, is believed to accelerate arteriosclerosis. Many packaged foods in our supermarkets contain large amounts of sugar, which pollute the taste buds, masking the true flavour of the food. Our taste buds are educated to expect this sweet pleasurable taste, in everything we eat. Our bodies become hooked on sugar and eventually, most foods not containing sugar, are considered awful in taste and are therefore shunned. Excessive sugar consumption is just as addictive as alcohol, nicotine and caffeine. These substances harm the consumer's health, in the long run. Caffeine is very addictive and when combined with large amounts of sugar, as it is in many canned drinks, is extremely detrimental to the future health of our children. Caffeine is an alkaloid drug, and we should discourage its use by our young children, so that they do not grow up dependent on their daily intake, to function effectively. This I believe is a very serious matter. In the affluent Western world, we are in great danger of becoming - if we are not already - dependent on our daily intake of these drugs. No wonder we pay scant attention to the natural world, and our destruction of the earth's resources. We are becoming like the drug addict, who will do anything to pay for his next fix. Like these poor souls, driven out of their minds, by a craving they cannot control, we seek only to please the senses, by obtaining more and more possessions and pleasurable experiences. And, most of us, are prepared to turn a blind eye, to the suffering that is incurred in the process.

The food we eat is of vital importance to our health, both physically and mentally and therefore spiritually. Your perception of the world and conditions surrounding you, will be severely coloured, by your addiction to the pleasures of eating.

If you eat to live, there is still pleasure in the consumption of your food, without the excessive addiction. The body will be nourished adequately, without having to deal with excesses that are a burden on the physical system. The mind will be freer from the constraints of the body's addiction, and able to appreciate the realities of the world and its surrounding to a larger degree. The greater harmony of body and mind, will ensure that the purification of the spirit is not unnecessarily hindered.

Finally an ascetic approach to diet, in my opinion, is

also incorrect. Food is provided by God, that we may nourish our bodies and replenish our energies. I believe we should enjoy these gifts, and give thanks. Eat to live and, not over indulge, or waste food. Because if we over indulge and waste food, while others go hungry elsewhere, how can man's spirit become free, to soar to new heights?,

You may agree or disagree with the opinions I have expressed here. You must make up your own mind; take responsibility for your diet. After all, if you lived in Iceland or were part of the Bedouin people, it would be rather difficult, if not impossible, to comply with the suggestions made here. However whether you agree or disagree with me, I hope I have given you food for thought.

~~~

Impressions And Expressions

What we see and how we interpret this is a very difficult process, because we are sentient beings and not merely mechanical machines. We have a body that is capable of mechanical movement, but we also have a tactile quality that allows us to feel what we touch with our bodies, we also have the ability to sense things. This ability to sense things without being in contact in any physical way, we often describe as intuition. Most of us have, at some time or other, experienced a tingling feeling on the back of the neck and an irresistible urge to turn round. And, as we turn round, we find our eyes look straight into the eyes of another person, who was staring at us from behind. Somehow we picked up the fact that someone was staring at us, our senses alerted; we felt an urgent need to turn in the direction of the other person. Something about us raised enough curiosity, in this other person, for them to focus their attention on us so strongly, that we felt the energy expressed by them. So we have at our disposal, the ability to move our body mechanically, to feel through touch, to perceive energies, to be intuitive.

We live in an increasingly technological age, where our references are becoming more and more influenced by computers and other modern scientific technological apparatus. Most of our references then are mechanical and so when we experience problems in the sentient side of life, often out of habit and conditioning, we apply the logical thought and solutions we have become practiced in while dealing with this mechanical environment. Which is unfortunate, because this is often inappropriate. We are, for better or worse, emotional beings and we need to take this into account, in our dealings with each other. Applying purely logical thought and solutions to human behaviour, without any consideration of our feelings and senses, must result in conflict. Machines can be expected to react to instructions logically, and given the same instructions, identical machines will react to the instructions in exactly the same way. Humans are unique, in that we not only have physical abilities, tactile qualities and senses at our disposal, but we also have the power of reason. And it is the combination of these capabilities; the mixing of these skills, that sets us ultimately above machines. For whilst machines can be made to perform a given task faster, or be imbued with a strength and power greater than any single human being, without humans to build and throw the switches to set the machines in motion, they would not, could not, exist. We must never fall prey to the belief that our highly technical machinery is sacrosanct, it is not. They are merely tools we have built and set in motion, to take care of repetitive and strenuous tasks, so that we are free to experience more creative use of our unique abilities.

The God given ability to use our intelligence to look at a situation or a condition and envisage it being different. And then set about making changes, taking actions that will produce something born out of our own imagination. This ability, is an extremely useful tool, and using this tool wisely can benefit mankind enormously. But like all things, this tool can be used for good or ill. The intention of the perpetrator of these activities, is the all-important factor. If the intention is embodied in the self, the ego, then whatever progress is made will be false. Because it will, of necessity, mean that someone suffers a loss, so that the other may show a gain. If this gain is then in part, or in total, passed on to others to enlist their support and allegiance, the result is the same. Some lose, so that others may benefit. This kind of behaviour only provides constant fuel to feed the fires of conflict, as each person's ego strives to gain a superior position, and thereby dominate the other. This behaviour, which I believe is all too prevalent in today's society, where everyone is conditioned to fight for a larger and larger piece of the universal cake, is I believe, a contributory factor for the great disharmony present around the world today. The solution, change the behaviour and you change the conditions which govern our intention during our communication with each other. Whether that communication is between individuals, groups, businesses, or from one political administration to another. If the intention is to improve the lot of human endeavour, by seeking to find benefit to both parties. Without one feeling that they have made a loss and the other a gain then the emotions and the ego are quelled. When a conclusion has been reached because both parties have received and given in acceptable measure, each parties equilibrium is maintained. Their mental and emotional state, produce a feeling of personal satisfaction and at the same time a feeling of contribution; a harmonious state follows.

How do we produce these obviously beneficial results? Who do we look to, to initiate the process? YOU AND I must do it. We have to look to ourselves and ask ourselves the question. How can I alter the way I communicate and interact with others, that will benefit both the other party and myself. We may be insignificant, as individuals. But if we can improve ourselves, take responsibility for our own actions, I believe we can, by this process, increase our usefulness in all of our relationships. Within our own families, at work and in our leisure time, spent in the company of our friends:

FROM LITTLE ACORNS, MIGHTY OAKS DO GROW.

By taking the responsibility for making an improvement within ourselves, which is the only way we can effectively alter the whole without inducing conflict, we serve, as do our subsequent actions, as an example to others. Showing by example, through our dealings with others, will allow them the opportunity to consider the improvement in our temperament and general demeanour. If we do nothing more than influence one or two other individuals in our entire life, along with encouraging our own children to approach adulthood with a greater compassion and a more caring nature, then we will have made a significant contribution. The more this happens, the greater will be the effect, for love is like knowledge, the more you give the more you will receive, and love like knowledge knows no bounds; they are both unlimited, infinite.

In the art of Tai Chi, the movements of beginners are all expressed through the outwards movement of arms, and generally, too much body motion. The reason for this, is that the outward signs of movement, the flowing of the peripherals, the arms, legs and body, are what are seen with the eyes. The motions of the practitioner are what the spectator sees, the physical actions. This is what the newcomer sees and therefore this, is what they try to emulate. The tactile sensations of the experienced Tai Chi practitioner and the sense (intuitive) abilities that are utilized, as they work their way through their routines, are hidden from view. As the beginners watch and then copy, all they have to go on is what they see, the mechanical movement, and in the beginning this is correct. Without attaining some degree of mastery over the physical movements of the body, the subtler abilities of feel and sense (intuition) are not connected and therefore in conflict with each other, rather than harmonizing together. The harmonizing of these abilities, produces a quality to their movements, which gives the experienced Tai Chi practitioners performance such a magically enthralling appearance.

Through constant practice the Tai Chi student learns to move from within. Instead of the centre, following the peripherals. Instead of the mind, focusing on the external appearance of the form and producing a robotic performance, an expression of the self (ego). Alternatively, with the mind cleared of one's own self importance, with the mind empty and clear like a pool of water, unrestricted, now the centre moves, and the peripherals follow, the arms, legs, become an expression of the movement within. In this way, one becomes an expression of the supreme spirit and the performance of the Tai Chi form becomes what it should be, moving meditation.

Logic dictates, that the quickest way from one point to another, is in a straight unbending line; whereas nature and the wise know, that this is not necessarily true. Having a destination and moving towards it, without taking into account changing conditions during your journey, makes it forced and fraught with danger. All in nature follows inborn patterns and instincts, all in nature moves to the conditions that surround it; and all in nature adapts to changing conditions, survival depends on flexibility. If there is a shortage of food in one area, animals in that area must move elsewhere to find food or perish. They do this without the ability to make logical analyses of the situation. Many species of birds and animals travel many hundreds of miles for reasons of shortages of food, a safer breeding place, or more suitable climatic conditions, and they do this using abilities for the most part, we humans do not fully understand.

Tai Chi, in accordance with the laws of nature, has no straight lines. The movements of the arms and legs, as well as that of the body, are all circular or curved, but these must be natural, not exaggerated. In fact, straight or flat is an illusion really. If you magnify any flat or straight material object enough, you will find that flat and straight are perceptual on our part, and this false perception is caused by our limited vision. I think it was Einstein who proved, that even light bends.

Earlier today, whilst out walking with Gisela, we had a thrilling and uplifting experience together. We decided to rest for a while, on a bench under the ruined castle that overlooks North Bay. The view there is magnificent and I go there often, as I find the view exhilarating. Spread in front of us was the vastness of the sea, then cliffs in the distance beyond the bay. Above us, great white clouds sailed across the deep blue sky, quite quickly too, as the wind was blowing very strongly today. Seagulls glided by, riding the winds. I moved my gaze periodically from the sea, to the cliffs and then the gulls, beautiful, truly beautiful. Gisela and I talked of our love for this place, and how fortunate we are to be able to enjoy such natural splendour. All free of charge, a gift from nature.

As I sat watching the sea, a bird glided into view to my right. I turned to watch it; it seemed motionless, as it hovered in mid air, riding the thermals. The bird was two hundred yards or so away from the cliffs and about three hundred yards to our right. I pointed in the direction of the bird and Gisela and I watched this master of the air. It appeared to be suspended in mid air, perfectly still without any effort at all. Then, for no apparent reason, it swooped down and glided round in a wide circle to its right, and stopped a little further back from its original position. Gisela and I were amazed at the speed with which the bird travelled. Below us, at the bottom of the cliffs, cars were traveling along the coast road and this gave us a contrasting view. The cars motion depends on much effort, many hours of hard labour went into making these vehicles;

much sweat is produced in getting the oil out of the ground. And then refining it, into the various lubricants and fuels, without which, these machines cannot move. And as we watched this master of the sky, ride the vernal winds above the automobiles below. Sweeping past them, at such incredible speed that they appeared to be virtually stationary, and then this amazing aerial magician stopped dead, it did not slow to a stop like the vehicles below do, it just stopped. One second, it was gliding at tremendous speed in an arc and then it was stationary, hovering again. We were full of admiration for this incredible feathered vertebrate, and as we watched and admired this beautiful creature, we discussed how we as humans, even with all our superior technology and greater brainpower, cannot match the majesty of movement of this superb natural king of the airwaves. After a few seconds, with the merest flap of its wings, it rose up on the air current and then glided forward to hover again. This time, this magnificent bird was only thirty yards or so, forwards of our position and hovering just slightly below us. Now we could see it more clearly, its back and the wings close to the body were a lovely brown colour, the rest of its wings were edged with black and it had a fanned tail in similar colours. It was thrilling to see it so close up, its beauty and aerial acrobatics where captivating, we watched it spellbound. Now the bird was closer, we could see that far from being totally motionless, the bird had to constantly monitor its position and make adjustments. It did this altering, by just a hint of movement to its wings or its body position, rolling slightly to the left or right and occasionally changing the angle of one of its wings. So when I thought it was stationary, as I watched it earlier, it was not motionless at all, I was merely deluded by my limited vision.

We continued to watch the bird as it hovered, suddenly it

flapped its wings frantically for a while, dropped down sharply, then rose up on a thermal circled round in a large arc and returned, more or less to the same position again. As I watched, I learned again. Another illusion shattered. I realized that before, when I thought the bird had swooped down for no apparent reason, and then glided round to hover again in more or less the same spot. That again, my lack of vision, had limited my comprehension. This aerial acrobat par excellence, knows that to resist the ways of nature is fruitless and saps precious, vital energy. So when the wind dropped, it flapped its wings to try to hold its position for a few seconds, in the hope that the wind would return. And when this was not forthcoming, rather than waste precious energy, it dropped until it connected with another thermal, where it could rise, bank, curving with the wind and return to its previous height again. Then, when the wind allows, should it choose to do so, it may return to its original position. This bird knows instinctively, it must work with the forces of nature, it knows, instinctively that to oppose the forces of nature is folly, inviting calamity and is fraught with danger. It has learnt to flow with the wind, a fundamental force within its environment. It adapts to naturally occurring conditions that call for change easily, without undue resistance. It follows the Tao (way) of its existence, its destiny, and within the confines of the prevailing conditions that surround it, because it does not resist the forces of nature, it has complete freedom: a true master of itself and of its environment. Checking a book on birds later, back at home, I learnt we had been watching a Kestrel.

Man, because he has been given the power to think, to reason, to analyse, to envisage, to produce concepts from his own mind, inherits with this power, the ability to imagine that he is greater than any other species. By our actions, we show that we believe that all the other inhabitants of the earth that get in our way, or oppose our progress are expendable; all must serve mankind and his insatiable lust for more and more prosperity. Man imposes his will upon all and therefore becomes "out of sink.," with the true nature of things. Unable to follow, his ego forces him to lead.

When I see such magnificent examples of nature's diversity and glorious beauty, such as Gisela and I were privileged to enjoy, whilst watching this incredible bird, so finely tuned to its environment. Then I have this feeling, that we were given this power of mental superiority so that we have the ability, should we choose to exercise it, to serve the earth and all its inhabitants. I believe we are the custodians of nature. When, in our greed, we cause the extinction of a species, we remove the opportunity to experience the wonder of nature in its natural state, and we all become poorer because of it. A better balance could perhaps be found, otherwise the only animals left for our children to experience, will be a computer image in a virtual reality machine and that would be sad, and a sure sign of self destruction.

Many creatures have physical capabilities beyond the scope of human capacity, capabilities we cannot match, even with all of our technology. They adapt and work with nature out of instinct, being devoid of our ability to analyse and reason, they follow the way of their own destiny, without complaints. As human beings, we have a choice; we can work with nature or try to manipulate it, for our own gain. But if in the process of manipulating whatever hinders or impedes our progress, we destroy species of plants, animals, birds and aquatic life, surely, we are reducing the quality of our own existence.

Instead, with this gift of thought, this unique human faculty, can we not see that to work with nature, to flow with the tide of life, to ride the winds of existence, is our natural heritage, our destiny. I believe we were meant to look and learn from nature, not destroy it. If we upset the ecosystem of our planet, we will perish with it, machines will not help us then. We need food and water as basic necessities of life, if we damage the earth's ecosystem to the point where these cannot be produced, we cannot survive. However, if instead we try to enhance, as against oppose, the natural living systems on our planet, it would seem to me we must elevate our existence and with it our spirits. Would this not promote happiness and ease, and is this not preferable to the aggression and anxiety, that is currently so rife in many parts of the world today?

Today I am back in my home town of Hull and out for a walk again. It is a pleasant day, the sun is shining and a strong breeze is blowing. This time, I take my walk through a wood, to some unused chalk pits that have been turned into a country park a few miles out of town. It is a few days before Easter and there are quite a few children playing here, paddling in the pools, riding bicycles, playing on the swings and climbing frames built out of wood and rope, there is much laughter to be heard here. I made my way up the steps that lead out of the quarry. On the top, overlooking that excavation, is a path through some more woods and a clearing with a picnic area, that sports two tables with benches, for people to eat at. As it was now late afternoon, few people came this way and I sat on one of the benches and watched the birds pop in and out of the woods, looking for food. Without the noise and the constant movement of people back and forth, the birds foraged around the tables searching for scraps of food left behind, they paid little attention to me, as I sat there quietly watching them. The sun was shining and there was only a slight breeze up there. The trees on the slopes above the quarry obstructed the strong winds, making it warm and comfortable; I lay back on the wooden bench and looked at the sky. It was a glorious mid blue colour, the clouds raced across it. I could not remember ever seeing the clouds move so fast, the smaller clouds were occasionally broken up by the ferocity of a sudden gust of wind. As I lay there surveying the movement of the clouds and the apparent stillness of the sky, the vibrancy of it all stirred me within. Out of the meditative state of my mind, focused as it was upon the sky, came thoughts with an agility that matched the swiftly moving clouds. Like the clouds, small thoughts came and were dispersed, by the ferocity of the constant and persistent evolutionary process of my mind as it watched, remembered, brought forth from the depths of my subconscious; saw in the present, searched my memory for information gleaned in the past, and from these produced thoughts, opinions, my individual insights.

Now another thought comes, something that does not disperse but expands. I remember Gisela explaining to me, after one of her art classes, how to paint the sky and clouds, you must be able to see the different colours in it. The sky is not merely blue or grey, but is often composed of hues of yellow and red, and the clouds are not merely white or grey, but often have tinges of blue, yellow and red in them. I remembered how amazed I was when she told me, not because of the fact that the information was new to me, but because I had been looking at the sky for many years and had never, until then, noticed the other colours. I had seen only the blue or grey sky and the white and Grey clouds. Yet now, as I looked at this gorgeous azure celestial sphere - because of this transfer of information - now I see more. The different hues were always there - available for all, including me, to see - nothing was hidden from me - only my limited understanding, which limited my vision and blinded me to the truth.

Up there in the sky, colours. Down below, in the landscape, with its many hues depicted by the light, and the shadows, with their variable shades and dark corners. In the behaviour of all living creatures, in the actions of the rivers and oceans, in fact, in everything under and including the sun; everything is there to see, nothing is hidden from us. The Tao (God) lays all knowledge before us, in the functioning of nature, but we do not always comprehend what we see. Our brains, fettered by what we know, cluttered by our deductions and discernment, are unable to see the simple truth.

Back in Scarborough a few days later, early in the morning Gisela and I went down to the harbour and had breakfast from a cafe in a caravan there, is was simple fare, a toasted teacake and a mug of tea. It was a spontaneous thought on Gisela's behalf and I have learnt to accept these, sometimes reluctantly. My nature is such that I believe in work first, play later. However, Gisela seems to know when I need to unwind and knowing I intended to write suggested a walk down to the harbour would be nice first, as the weather was so warm. So off we went, hand in hand, out into the sunshine. We are indeed extremely lucky, to live in such a beautiful place.

Having purchased our teas and teacakes, we walked along the harbour wall a little way past some early morning fishermen. Then settled down, dangling our feet over the harbour wall, as we ate our teacakes and drank our tea, it was great. Then we lay down to enjoy the morning sun and I stared out across the bay, no boats in sight, just the sea and the sky. A little while later, I turned to look at the castle above the town and the cliff on which it stands. Then I turned my attention to the houses to the left of the castle, tiered up the side of the hill, and as I looked at the houses thoughts of people, situations, expectations and plans entered my mind and I spoke of these with Gisela. We talked for a little while and then I cast my gaze back across the bay and my mind became quiet again. Whilst I looked at this great expanse of water below and the open sky above, somehow it seemed impossible for me to think, I could only look. Gisela spoke to me and when she had finished I relayed my realisation to her, that whilst I looked towards the sea, which had nothing on it to distract my mind, my thoughts ceased. Yet when I turned and looked towards the town, with its expression of culture and civilization, thoughts were immediately born in my mind. I asked Gisela, if she thought everyone ceased to think when they looked at nature, without any material distractions. Gisela said she thought many people superimpose an image, over the purity of nature, and this draws their mind and keeps it busy. I realised that I used to be like that (still am sometimes), but through my training in the Taoist Arts of Tai Chi and self defense, I have learnt to quieten my mind under certain conditions and just look. Without judging or analysing what I see, just observing and experiencing. For me, this is the best kind of meditation, the vastness and beauty of nature quells the stress, brought on by the trammel of existence, like no other leisure activity can.

Perhaps one day, I will be able to stop in this meditative state permanently, and then restriction and stress will not exist for me. Then I will be a perfect instrument of the supreme spirit, where my every action and thought will not be mine at all, but the supreme spirits (but I won't hold my breath while I am waiting). In the meantime, I get an impression of what I should do and I express myself as best I can. I practice and teach Tai Chi and the other Taoist Arts, and write about my understanding of these and how they relate to everyday life. I realise that I still know so little, yet I can only contribute by offering what I have. No one can give what they do not possess and we all, all of us, through our unique experiences of life, have something to offer. Find out what yours is and then give it in full measure, hold nothing back, and believe me, you will be rewarded beyond your wildest dreams.

As often as I can, I get out amongst nature and look, listen and learn. Through teaching the Taoist Arts, I interact with people and from this, I learn much about human behaviour and my own shortcomings. It is a fascinating, exciting life and I am truly grateful, for all that I receive. I am lucky I have found my way. Look inward to yourself and you can find yours. But be patient as nature is, must be. For the ocean cannot control the tides, the earth cannot control the amount of sunshine bestowed upon it. These things are provided by the Tao. Be receptive, be still, empty yourself, only then can gifts be given to you. There is an old Taoist saying:

BE PATIENT AND YOU WILL ACHIEVE ALL THINGS

~~~

Today

Today is the most beautiful day in your life, today holds the most exciting possibilities you will ever experience; OR today is the worst day of your life, today is the most boring day you can ever remember. The choice is yours.

Some years ago I spent a few days with my master, Chee Soo, whilst he and his wife Marilyn, enjoyed a short break in Scarborough. During this time, he spoke to me of destiny. I listened carefully to all he said and now, as I enjoy a walk through the countryside, as I pause to look at some lovely wild flowers and appreciate their fragrance, I am reminded of these conversations.

WHEN YOU ASK FOR NOTHING MORE THAN THAT WHICH YOU ARE GIVEN,

ONLY THEN WILL YOU BE TRULY HAPPY AND CONTENT.

To grow, these flowers need nutrients from the earth, our mother. The roots take what is presented to them, without judging the food good or bad for they have neither the reasoning power to do so, nor any choice in the matter. The seeds, scattered by the wind, grow where they can, if they land on fertile soil they flourish, if they land on poor soil they struggle to survive or perish. The seeds have no knowledge of what they will become.

WE are flowers in Gods garden, and special ones at that, because God has given us the power of reason. Unfortunately, this power of reason also allows us to analyse the past and present, and then foolishly we predict the future. If the future does not meet our expectations, we see this as a restriction, a problem. Yet this problem was of our own making, for we created it, out of our own minds. Our power of reason, I believe, was given to us, so that we may consciously come to know all we have is in the present. The future is a pattern only God can weave. Our power of reason is to deal with the external structuring of life. The internal, our path, the Tao of our own lives, is to unresistingly follow Gods will, the Way. We can disobey Gods commands, because we have the power of reason, to make choices in our physical lives. But we CANNOT oppose his will, we cannot change the spiritual path we must follow, but we can effectively slow down the process. Ideally we can accept what we are given and not judge it good or bad, for all is beautiful, only we create ugliness. For in Gods creation, there can only be beauty.

On our journey through life we meet many others, and we each nourish each other. Often, seeing the opportunity for growth, we attach ourselves to others. Then God who placed us close together, sometimes replants again and puts distance between us. He has no wish to create suffering, he only weaves his pattern. Whilst we are together, we feed and nourish each other. But, as our diet changes, as we mature, so God in his greater wisdom changes our spiritual needs, so that we may continue to grow and develop in our own special way.

So, just as these flowers that I gaze upon, have a beauty that is unique, so too do you. Accept the food you are given, accept the environment and conditions surrounding you, accept the present, enjoy it, seek not to dwell on the negative but look for and experience the positive, it is there if you look. It is not possible to have absolute Yin without any Yang present. If your present conditions and environment seem difficult, do your best to remain cheerful and go about your business in a pleasant manner. The tide of life will come along and smooth the sands, washing them clean, bringing fresh nutrients to revitalize and energize. When the tide comes in, perhaps you will decide to board a boat for different climes, ride the waves to new exciting places. New experiences await you, whether you cross the sea or travel overland; you do not even have to travel, if you choose not to do so, but you must embrace the new. You must move forwards, you cannot remain immobile, to stand still is to stagnate. To stagnate is to lack life, to become dull. Everything in nature is in constant flux, ever changing, ever moving forwards.

Nothing in nature complains about its conditions and environment. Either the conditions and environment are accepted, or if they are unfavourable for survival, then movement to a new area is seen not as a negative solution that upsets the status quo, but as a positive opportunity to continue life. If you choose to hide away like a hermit or stay within your tiny select little group, never mixing with others, never venturing to new unknown places, complaining that it is dangerous to involve yourself with the unknown. Then fear controls your behaviour, life is not dealing you a bitter blow; you are limiting yourself. Take courage, meet new people, go to new places. Sure, sometimes things will not be pleasant, you may even get hurt physically or emotionally, but YOU WILL BE LIVING. And life will be exciting, joyful, you will learn much and contribute much.

You will perhaps be a little frightened occasionally, but happier than you have ever been before. God, The Tao, whatever name you prefer to use for the supreme spirit, has given you the most wonderful gift, life, so live it. The best way to repay the debt for this most precious bequest, is to live life to the full.

During my training in the Taoist arts, I have learnt that fear is the most limiting factor in my personal development. Fear to try things or practise what I find difficult. I am reminded again of that apt prayer:

LORD ALLOW ME THE HUMILITY TO ACCEPT THE THINGS I CANNOT CHANGE.

THE COURAGE TO CHANGE THE THINGS THAT OUGHT TO BE CHANGED.

AND THE WISDOM TO KNOW THE DIFFERENCE.

I am fortunate indeed, to have had the honour of being a student of a true Master, those past twenty one years. He's now, long departed from this physical realm. I am left to be the orchestrator of my own improvement. Yet because of the knowledge he imparted to me, over the years, in the latter part of his life, when I was close to him, I learnt much more, than in the previous years. Simply because I asked less questions, and listened more. When in his company or watching him demonstrate a technique, I paid more attention than before. I saw more, because there was less of me getting in the way and obscuring the truth. And because of what I learnt, I now teach. For if you truly want to receive, then you must first give. The Yin comes before the Yang always, this is the natural order of things and because I recognize this simple truth, I teach so that I may learn more. I do my best to follow the example of my Master, who was always a servant to his students, for a master does not dominate; a true Master only serves.

~~~

Is Anyone In?

Has anyone ever said that to you, when you were engrossed in your own thoughts? Whilst trying to attract your attention or talking to you, they suddenly realise that you are not aware of their efforts, to draw your consideration. Then standing directly in front of you, raising their voice or touching you, they manage to reach your consciousness and then jokingly they say 'Hello is there anyone in'.

Some people practise meditation techniques for hours every day, to obtain the ability to focus their attention to this degree. Of course there is an essential difference here: in the first instance, we have someone engrossed in some thought that entered into the mind, and then the mind thinks about it, expands it, analyses it and in the process, loses contact with their other senses to a large degree. Often, whilst in this state accidents happen, sometimes minor ones like walking into a lamppost, or stepping into a puddle and getting your feet soaking wet. On other occasions, these lapses in concentration cause people to walk out into the road in front of motor vehicles, or cause themselves serious injury in some other way. Whereas those who sit in contemplation, have a conscious wish which is quite the opposite of the above: in this second instance, we have people who remove themselves to a quiet place, away from the hustle and bustle of everyday life. Where they can relax and become in touch with themselves, without the extraneous distractions which in most of us, so easily draw the mind, like a magnet draws iron filings. In this tranquil setting, devoid of external stimulus, the body can be taught to relax, the mind can be brought under control.

What do we mean by, bringing the mind under control? Is it not already under our control? Well in my experience as a teacher of Tai Chi and self-defense, the answer with most people, has to be a definite no. Unless the person has had training, in some area that requires control of the mind, so that it can be focused at will on a particular activity. Then concentration, coupled with self-awareness, for most people, is an extremely difficult thing to achieve.

So do I advocate sitting in a quiet room, trying to still the mind in order to bring it under control, Yes and No. Yes I think it has value, for those who need to learn how to relax, and yes accompanied by watching the breathing, preferable abdominal breathing, I believe it has great value in quietening the mind. However for those people who find it difficult to sit quiet and relax, then no, for those people this is a pointless exercise. First they must be conditioned to a lack of activity by some sort of gradual slowing down process, some process that does not include strenuous activity. But one that involves some form of gentle activity, so that mind has something to be busy with - ENTER 'TAI CHI' AND THE SOFT ARTS OF KUNG FU SUCH AS 'FENG SHOU'. Those people who cannot concentrate for long, will not be attracted to Tai Chi, finding it too slow for their temperament. These people would be better advised to practise the soft arts of Kung Fu such as 'Feng Sau' which means 'Hand of the Wind'.

Let us assume, however, that we are able to concentrate for a while and find the movements of Tai Chi fascinating and enchanting enough to want to know more. How can Tai Chi help us take control of our minds? Well not only will Tai Chi help you control your mind, it will improve your physical condition whatever your age, teach you correct natural breathing and increase your awareness of your own body. Thereby educating you to your own limitations and discovering and extending your abilities both mentally and physically.

Because whilst the exercises of Tai Chi are gentle in application, they are dynamic in their effect on the body and mind.

When a student has learnt a few movements of the Tai Chi form, they are introduced to the breathing pattern, that accompanies the slow, graceful, ballet like maneuvers. Previously, before the breathing was introduced, the movement of hands and feet are synchronized into an even pattern, that feels good, and when a degree of proficiency is gained, is aesthetic in appearance. Now the student has to learn to incorporate the correct breathing pattern, breathing in on the odd numbers or inward movements, and out on the even or outwards movements. This conforms to the principles of the Yin and Yang, the two naturally opposing, yet harmonious, primary elements emanating from the Tao.

The student soon encounters a problem, for example, the outward (breathing out) movement may be a short one. Followed by an inward (breathing in) movement, that is rather longer. Having learnt to regulate and even out the physical movement of arms and legs, the student naturally tries to continue this process, when the breathing pattern is introduced. Movements that are roughly equal cause no problems. But then suddenly, by comparison, a short movement followed by a much longer movement, brings confusion, and alongside it, the temptation to force things. This even pattern we have been observing, which has served us well, suddenly, abruptly, causes problems. For as we execute a short movement whilst breathing out, we have not fully emptied the lungs and now following our even pattern, we start to breathe in again. Quickly filling the lungs to maximum capacity, yet we should, because of our even pattern, still be taking an inwards breath. As our lungs are full, we have nowhere to store this breath, we cannot hold our breath, because the breathing should follow the same rhythmic pattern, as do our movements. At first this seems as unsolvable problem.

Let us examine the problem. We must keep a nice even measured flow, in both our bodily maneuvers and also our breathing. Our difficulty is due mostly to our ability to use logic, our brains prefer logical, structured patterns that can be analysed and reapplied, to solve similar solutions, over and over again. However, as nature shows us with the natural world and the phenomenon within, there is a chaotic natural order. That we and all living creatures must accept, if we are to live in harmony with ourselves, and each other. After all, does not day follow night, in an unending perpetual rhythm and the seasons follow each other, with each cycle in the same order as the last? But who amongst us, can regulate night and day to an even pattern with each the same length in hours and minutes, and who amongst us, can regulate the seasons in the same way? NOBODY! There is a pattern to be seen, but not one amongst us can alter it. We must see it, accept it, and follow it. By working within its framework, following its principles, we can maintain our equilibrium, be in harmony with the cosmos. When we oppose this natural order, we become discordant with the way and disruption and disorder will follow, as surely as night follows day. And there is the crux of our problem, with our Tai Chi form. For to learn the true essence of Tai Chi, one must learn to see the pattern, experience the flow, give oneself up to it, work with it, and then most importantly. As ones knowledge and understanding strengthened, and new elements are introduced, we must learn to be adaptable.

A good instructor will gently lead his students down the path he has travelled himself, guiding, encouraging and sometimes chiding, until the correction process by the teacher is eventually replaced, by the students own observation and perception. Self awareness has now been placed squarely at the learners feet, so to speak. Now, not only have they the external information about their movements, passed on to them by their instructor. But, they now have their own experience, they know what they feel like, as they perform the Tai Chi movements. Instead of only looking outwards and receiving feedback from others, as to the quality of their Tai Chi, they are now looking inwards and feeling, becoming aware of the inner, as well as the outer. A more balanced view is obtained, and their Tai Chi enters the realm of moving meditation. Some people give up before they reach this stage, which is a great shame, because the benefits to one's everyday life, is beyond normal comprehension.

All over the country, there are many seminars being held now, that offer to increase our self-awareness. These courses cover a diverse range of subjects and I am not qualified to comment on the validity of the material, or its value to enhance the perception of the individuals attending them. My understanding of the sentient, the tactile quality of my life, has been promoted through the auspices of the Taoist Arts, and my own individual life experience so far. However, I would like to say, that my own acquittance from the daily round of selfishly seeking more and more private prosperity, at the expense of my personal happiness, has been gained through participation. That is to say, knowledge gained through books, colleges, seminars and ones individual life experiences has, I believe, to be put into use in some practical physical sense. Otherwise it is merely intellectual fantasy, and as such, can have no relevance to our self-development as human beings. Existing as we do and drawing knowledge - real knowledge is -

from our own direct experience, our everyday actions in the real world. Not a hypothesis, a hypothetical analytical appraisal, but authentic genuine actions, committed in reaction to the physical world we live in. This may well be a world of illusion. But it is where we are right now, and as such, is our only reality. For better or worse we live in the present, along with all else in nature. The further we move into the past or future, the further we move away from life. Think about it and then ask yourself the question. "Hello is there anyone in?"

~~~

Freedom

Speaking out, campaigning for the freedom of others, devising fierce arguments, taking violent action, this is futile. You cannot gain true freedom for others, by forcible and aggressive means. People can only gain true freedom for themselves. We are born, in whatever country our destiny places us. However, if we are fortunate enough to have plenty, we have the freedom of choice to give food, money and our time, to help those with fewer resources than ourselves. The Tao (The Way) does not forbid us to show compassion for our fellow man.

I believed in freedom so strongly, I pursued it so stubbornly, I became a prisoner to it, a slave within my own freedom.

Is it possible to have too much freedom? Yes! I think it is. If one has no routine to abide by, no discipline to adhere to, imposed or self imposed, then it is easy to lose ones direction and become lost in one's own precious freedom. Speaking from my own experience. I find that with a goal to work towards, I can formulate a plan to obtain the desired effect, this creates a discipline, which in turn creates movement. But why do we need to do anything? Well if we do nothing at all, what benefit can we obtain from living this life, we have been granted. Surely we were born for a reason, so that we could contribute in some way, to human existence.

Learning to reach inwards, to harmonize the body and mind with the spirit, is the only true freedom. For then, all the mundane things of life, are taken care of. Learn to follow your own personal Tao (way), guided by your spirit, and your life will take on a new meaning. As you learn to follow your own personal destiny, your bearing will transform, others will see the joy you are experiencing, the happiness and pleasure that surrounds you in your work, your contribution to the pot.

Whatever your endeavours at work and in your personal life, be patient; for fast external growth, leads to internal weakness. If the foundations of a house are poor, the external structure will soon crumble. Over feed the body and exercise too little, or too much, and weakness will appear internally, within the organs of the system, then degeneration of the outside will surely follow. The surest way to keep the exterior of the body sound is to nurture the inner. In other words, start at the beginning. This is true in all spheres of life. Learn Tai Chi movements too fast, and quality will be lacking.

For many years I was working as a salesman, and from this, I learnt that if you did not capture the customer's interest with your initial opening statements, that their attention would quickly start waning. I know that if I start to read a book and the first few pages do not arouse my interest, then I am unlikely to read further.

So it seems to me, that the beginning of any venture, is of extreme importance. At work or at home, or in your leisure activities, when you start something, you set the perimeters of your experience. If you decide the task is going to be difficult, awkward, unpleasant or boring, it will be so, how could it be any other way; you willed it. You do however, have the freedom of choice, and you can, at the beginning choose to create the atmosphere in which you will dwell, as you tackle your task. Even if the task is set for you, as for example, in your work place, you can still choose the attitude that will reign. You have the freedom to control yourself, within the restriction of the conditions and the surroundings that you are placed in. And if you really cannot do your work without hating it, then change your job; your health depends on it. Being miserable, unhappy and ill tempered at work all day, will see you arriving home in a depressed state to greet your family, not conducive to a happy home life, in the long term.

To be truly free, one needs to be adaptable. Without the ability to adapt to changing circumstances, ones behaviour must become restrictive, in relation to the immediate environment and conditions. This restriction must produce conflict internally, and then our anger is often taken out, on the material object that is handy. We have all kicked the car or banged the TV etc., in pure frustration at some time, or other. When there is another human being involved and things are not going our way, we enter into conflict with them and if unable to bully them into our way of thinking, then often we indulge ourselves in a mental struggle for power. Manipulating information and events, to add credence to our argument, we waste precious energy in a non productive way.

If we are to live life to the full, we must intermingle with our own species, if we intermingle with our own species we will inevitably form relationships, if we form relationships we must adapt to the other person or persons, to ensure a harmonious equilibrium within that relationship. If we have to adapt or compromise, is this not a loss of freedom? I used to hold that view, believing that to have to change ones plans or opinions, was a denial of my own personal liberty. However, as I have journeyed along my path, I have had reason to ponder previously firmly held beliefs, often changing an opinion here and there, and the above is one of them. I now believe, that the relationships we have with our family, wife or husband, children and friends etc., are the most important thing; much, much more precious, than the striving for material wealth or intellectual knowledge.

We all need to cultivate a little solitude for ourselves, to reach within and find out who we really are. But we exist in a world of many, and need that interconnection with others, so that we may expand as individuals. To me life is not like turning the pages of a book, but more of an unfolding, like the flower in spring or the journey of the stream down to the sea. It cannot be foretold or planned; only experienced, lived. Like the seed in the ground, knows not what it will become, and the stream, which knows not, where its journey will take it. The itinerary we will pass through, on our journey through life, is hidden from us. Like the seed grows and blooms according to the seasons, it has no control over nature, but the forces of nature control its development, and the stream that grows to become a river, collecting more substance, as it journeys along its route, but has no control over the path it must take. The ever changing elements of our lives, dictate our future, we only have the possibility to control such a small portion, namely the conditions that exist in the present, and the effects of any action we take, will have repercussions we never envisage.

Forming relationships with others and adapting to their presence, without demanding changes in their behaviour, to make the environment more suited to your usual practise, requires patience and adaptability. Giving up what you do not need, will encourage those close to you, to do the same. Until eventually, you work together, for the sake of the relationship and its survival. Each caring for each other, because you know they care for you. In your efforts to secure comfort and security within the relationship for the other members, you guarantee it for yourself. Gaining further, freedom in the process.

~~~

Is It Misty Today?

Gisela woke me up full of excitement today. Having got up earlier, she had looked out of the window to find the weather dull and a heavy mist covering the sea front. Disappointed, because she fancied an early morning walk down to the harbour, she went about her business. A little over an hour later, the mist cleared and she came to wake me, thrilled at the change in the weather. Her enthusiasm was infectious, so up I got and a little while later we were off to the harbour. It was a lovely sunny July day and as we walked, we talked of how beautiful everything was and what a good summer we were having this year. Once at the harbour, Gisela bought us a mug of tea and a teacake each and we strolled along the harbour wall to our favourite spot, where we settled down to enjoy our treat and the spectacular view.

Later, I lay down on the harbour wall, rested my head against Gisela's legs and enjoyed the sun. There was a slight breeze and as I lay there, with my shorts on and T-shirt off, the air flowed over my body like a gentle massage, relaxing my somatic structure, which had the effect of calming my mind. I looked at the cliff, on which the ruins of the castle stood. Mind and body soothed by the gentle summer breeze, no thoughts marred my tranquil disposition. My brain did not analyse what it saw, sedated by nature's elements, unruffled by the ravages of society, it was still. I could only look and see, nothing more, nothing less.

'Howard look,' cried Gisela, pointing out to sea.

Returning to the sentient world again, I looked in the direction she motioned me. The sight which confronted me, stunned me into silence. In my half conscious, half meditative state, words seemed erroneous, as my mind fought to comprehend the sight before it.

'Isn't that amazing,' Gisela said, staring out to sea.

A dense mist was moving towards the shore, at incredible speed. Watching it move rapidly towards us, filled us both with a feeling of consternation. Sat there on the harbour wall peering out to sea, watching it hastily disappear, totally enveloped by the advancing mist. As if devoured, by some great, uncontrollable, unstoppable beast. I would be a liar, if I said I felt no trepidation at the realisation, that this force of nature was beyond my control, all I could do was watch it, let it happen, and observe.

'Scary isn't it,' Gisela said.

'Yes,' I replied.

It was only a few hundred yards from the harbour wall now and closing fast.

'I bet it will be cold, when it reaches us,' Gisela said,

'Shall we go, or do you want to stay?'

'Let's stay,' I said, 'It will be an interesting experience.'

As I looked out to sea again, captivated by the incoming fateful haze, I saw a seagull glide right into the mist and then out again. It seemed this enormous white beast, that was ravenously consuming everything in its path, held no fear for this small sea bird. Again, and then once more it glided into the mist and out again, before it disappeared from sight as Neptune's breath swept over us and obscured it from view. The ghostly cloud surrounded us and moved past, to blur the boats close to the harbour wall and eclipse those, and anything else more than fifteen yards away. It was eerie on that wall, with everything within fifteen yards or so adumbrative and anything beyond dulled into obscurity. I glanced up towards the cliff and castle ruins, but they were totally obliterated by the thick fog. I tried to imagine what the view looked like, but the mist somehow obfuscated my mind. Physically, completely surrounded by the mist outside, somehow it seemed to penetrate my head and stupefy my mental processes.

Surprisingly enough low down, close to the harbour wall, it was not cold, the suns rays reached through the mist and brought us warmth. That warmth from the sun, that could not be seen, only felt, lifted the fear that the dense blanket had laid over my mind, bewilderment slowly receded and again I regained control of my intellect. Which the mist, producing as it did, fear of the unknown, had robbed me of. As I lay there, I wondered if I could have coped as bravely with this experience, had I been alone. I came to the conclusion I would not have, and would probably have walked back along the harbour wall to the sea front, terra firma and the illusion of security, which comes from the company of a crowd. However, with my lovely soul mate Gisela by my side, I am stronger when events in my life disturb my personal equilibrium and I recover, quicker because of her presence on my path. We came together by the will of the Tao and hand in hand, we journey down our path into the mist, we know not where, the destination is hidden from us and we can only see a little way ahead. But the journey is the thing that matters, it is so exciting, so much joy do we experience along the way, that we accept the difficult times, the occasional financial hardships and family problems with good humour, and endeavour not to become too melancholy, during such periods.

The cliffs and the castle ruins, the boats in the harbour, the ships out at sea, the seagulls and the sea front teeming with tourists, all these are still there, hidden for the time being from my view, but never the less still there; behind the mist.

I was reminded again of the affinity between the chaotic essence of nature and of our existence here on earth. I was reminded of those times in my life when the sun shone brightly, life was easy and all was well, and then suddenly out of the blue, an event took place that changed everything. And as I saw things gathering momentum and tried to stop the oncoming disastrous mutability, that was detrimental to my personal plans and aspirations, I was drawn into conflict with the way, into opposition to the Tao of my own life.

One can disobey the laws of nature, but one cannot change its inherent will. So my actions to alter the Tao of my life, when it enters a Yin phase, is as futile as trying to stop the flow of the mist, as it rolls off the sea onto the land, merely because it does not suit my mood. I may as well try to turn back the tide, as king Canute did. If I had been able to adapt more readily to the altering situation, instead of opposing it, the transformation of my development would have been smoother, less volatile. I have heard it said and I believe it to be true, that we are the cause of our own problems.

Fear plays a great part, in our resistance to change. Fear of the unknown. We make plans and have dreams, and surely having been given the reasoning power to do this by God, then surely this cannot be wrong. Where we often go wrong I feel is, in sticking too rigidly, to our original intentions. When changes occur that we did not envisage, instead of being mentally pliable and modifying our plans to take into account the variables introduced, erroneously we try to force our primary plan to work. Because we are comfortable with what we believe we can control, we feel safe. Even being deep in contention, we think, is better than dealing with our fear of the unknown. Yet we see all around us and constantly in nature, that life is spontaneous. Do plants complain, when winter stunts their growth and causes them to lay dormant? No! they accept it graciously and wait patiently for spring. Yin follows Yang, as night follows day, but the periods of each cannot be measured by the hours on a clock. Each must wait for the conditions in which it can flourish to appear, by the will of the Tao (the Way).

Forced growth will lead to weakness, only a slow natural ripening, will produces a strong healthy plant. We drain the strength of our food by speeding its natural cycle of growth, and then consuming these weakened foods, we are surprised at the increasing sickness that develops. I watched a programme on television the other day, about veterinary surgeons, and do you know the first question they always asked the owner of the sick animal? They ask 'What have you been feeding it on?' I have never personally, ever heard of anyone, being asked by their doctor, what they eat. Next time you are ill, you may be better off paying a visit to the local vet, rather than the doctor. We try to live life at such a fast pace these days, trying to cut corners on all of life's natural processes, cramming in as many of life's pleasures as possible, that we unnecessarily shorten our allotted span, through illness. Physically, by abusing our bodies, or mentally, by suffering too much stress and withdrawing from the spiritual side of life.

Anyway, back to my problem, my fear of the unknown. I remembered the seagull flying in and out of the mist, as it moved towards the shore. To the seagull, this experience was not a new one, it has experienced this phenomenon before many times, perhaps while still young seen its parents or peers disappear into the strange milky haze and then emerge again, unscathed and unperturbed. To Gisela and I, separated from land and any visible signs of civilization, way out from the shore, on the harbour wall, this was a new experience neither of us was acquainted with, and it was this unfamiliar situation that triggered our apprehension.

I have learnt that fear is the most inhibiting factor in my self development, in my enjoyment of life's rich tapestry, of the infinite opportunities to savour the true nectar of existence as a human being. For the remainder of my days, the only thing I have to fear, is fear itself. So when I encounter fear, I endeavour not to run away, as I did in the past, but to turn and face my fear. For, only by tasting that fear can I know it, if I turn and run, it remains the unknown. This does not mean I have a morbid fascination with fear, and go looking for situations that produce it. But rather, when confronted with fear, if I can steel myself to experience it, to examine it, I can get to know it, for we do not fear that which we know and understand. To hide from trepidation, to foolishly deny its actuality, is to nourish its growth. To see your fear, feel it, scrutinize it, to accept it, is to annihilate it.

~~~

The End

ABOUT THE AUTHOR

Howard grew up in Hull, East Yorkshire, England. After leaving school at 15yrs old, he started work: first as an apprentice welder – he was sacked for playing football too long in his lunch break. He then joined Halfords as a trainee manager, again being sacked for 'bad mouthing' the temporary manager (a right &*^"!) whilst the permanent manager (an okay guy) was on holiday. Going to the other extreme he joined the Army and served in Berlin and Aden (twice) during his six years.

Years later, as he was running his own shower installation business, he developed an interest in the Taoist Arts of Tai Chi and Feng Shou Kung Fu, becoming a student of the late Grand Master Chee Soo for twenty-one years. Through dedicated practice and regular personal training with Chee Soo Howard was awarded the highest grade issued by the Grand Master. Howard has been a practitioner of these fascinating arts since 1973 and has made a personal commitment to pass on the teachings he has received in a way that he feels follows the true spirit of the Arts.

The Taoist Arts have taught him that he is the master of his own personal journey.

He is blessed with having met his perfect woman along this path to share his life with, Gisela, his artist wife, who shows him the pinks in the sky.

Howard's Website can be seen at: www.howardgibbon.com

Printed in Great Britain
by Amazon.co.uk, Ltd.,
Marston Gate.